SERIES EDITOR: MARTIN WINDROW

ELITE 71

QUEEN VICTORIA'S COMMANDERS

TEXT BY
MICHAEL BARTHORP

COLOUR PLATES BY
DOUGLAS N. ANDERSON

D0898464

OSPREY
MILITARY

First published in 2000 by Osprey Publishing,
Elms Court, Chapel Way, Botley, Oxford OX2 9LP, United Kingdom

ISBN 1 84176 054 4

Editor: Martin Windrow
Design: Alan Hamp
Originated by Grasmere Digital Imaging Ltd, Leeds, UK
Printed in China through World Print Ltd

00 01 02 03 04   10 9 8 7 6 5 4 3 2 1

FOR A CATALOGUE OF ALL TITLES PUBLISHED BY OSPREY MILITARY,
AUTOMOTIVE AND AVIATION PLEASE WRITE TO:
The Marketing Manager, Osprey Publishing Ltd, PO Box 140,
Wellingborough, Northants NN8 4ZA, United Kingdom
Email: **info@ospreydirect.co.uk**

The Marketing Manager, Osprey Direct USA, PO Box 130,
Sterling Heights, MI 48311-0310, USA
Email: **info@ospreydirectusa.com**

Or visit the Osprey website at: **www.ospreypublishing.com**

Acknowledgements

The author gratefully acknowledges the assistance, in various ways,
of the following:
Douglas N.Anderson, Robin Barthorp, Mrs Desirée Battye,
Dr Margaret Bruce, Mrs Sara Crosby, Lieutenant-Colonel M.J.Evetts
MC, Lieutenant-Colonel A.A.Fairrie, Philip Haythornthwaite,
Anthony Higgins, Colonel P.J.Mercer, John Mollo,
Lieutenant-Colonel D.J.Murray, the Secretary of the East India Club,
Colonel D.R.Wood, and Miss Clare Wright of the National Army
Museum.

Glossary of Orders & Decorations

Orders and decorations mentioned in this book are as follows:
Victoria Cross (VC)
Order of St Patrick - Knight (KP)
Order of the Bath - Knight Grand Cross (GCB), Knight
    Commander (KCB), Companion (CB)
Order of the Star of India - Knight Grand Commander (GCSI),
    Knight Commander (KCSI), Companion (CSI)
Order of St Michael & St George - Knight Grand Cross (GCMG),
    Knight Commander (KCMG), Companion (CMG)
Order of the Indian Empire - Knight Grand Commander (GCIE),
    Knight Commander (KCIE), Companion (CIE)
Distinguished Service Order (DSO)

Artist's Note

Readers may care to note that the original paintings from which the
colour plates in this book were prepared are available for private
sale. All reproduction copyright whatsoever is retained by the
Publishers. All enquiries should be addressed to:

Douglas N.Anderson, 37 Hyndland Road,
Glasgow G12 9UY, Scotland

The Publishers regret that they can enter into no correspondence
upon this matter.

QUEEN VICTORIA'S COMMANDERS

INTRODUCTION

SUCCESS OR FAILURE IN WARFARE depends upon many factors but one of the most obvious is the calibre of the commanders, those who lead and direct the troops and operations – be they commanding an army, a corps, division, brigade or a regiment or some other formation, large or small. The aim of this work is to examine some of the more memorable – for one reason or another – of those who led the soldiers of the British Empire between 1837 and 1901, the reign of Queen Victoria, when that Empire reached the height of its fame and prestige.

The 64 years of Queen Victoria's reign saw the British Army engaged in three major conflicts: the only war against a European power, Russia, from 1854 to 1856 in the Crimea; the Indian Mutiny or Sepoy Revolt, from 1857 to 1859; and the war in South Africa against the two Boer Republics from 1899 to 1902. In addition there were nearly 70 other campaigns and expeditions all over the world, from Canada to New Zealand, of which at least half were fought in, or were mounted from, India. The first military operations began in the year of the Queen's accession, countering a rebellion in Canada; but the first proper war erupted one year later with an invasion of Afghanistan to forestall a perceived Russian threat against the territories of British India. These were then, and until 1860, administered and defended by the

The Victorian commanders' fighting arms – horse, foot and guns: types of regimental officers and men of the British Army in full dress between 1837-97. Print after R.Simkin. (Author's collection)

Honourable East India Company (HEIC) with its own three armies of Bengal, Madras and Bombay plus, from 1849, the Punjab Irregular (later Frontier) Force. All these were locally raised with British officers, supplemented by some European infantry and artillery units, and supported by regiments of the Queen's Army[1].

The higher commanders, those responsible for formations above regimental level, were ranked, in descending order of seniority, as: field-marshal, general, lieutenant-general, major-general, brigadier-general and colonel[2]. Their formations would consist of a descending number of regiments, cavalry and/or infantry, supported by batteries of artillery, companies of engineers and, in the latter half of the period, by elements of the logistic services – supply, transport, medical, ordnance etc.

The regiments were normally commanded by lieutenant-colonels, assisted by two majors and sometimes a second lieutenant-colonel. Their squadrons, companies or batteries were captains' commands, each with two subalterns (lieutenants or cornets/ensigns[3]). Between these company, or equivalent, officers and their men in the ranks stood the non-commissioned-officers, various grades of sergeant and corporals. NCOs, in strict military terminology, cannot be classed as commanders. Nevertheless, in Kipling's words, they were 'the backbone of the Army', and when their officers fell it was they who took command of the soldiers and did their utmost to 'lift them through the charge that wins the day'[4]. In recognition of their worth three will be met later in these pages, two of them being among the few NCOs who were commissioned for distinguished service in the field.

Commanders at all levels would be assisted by staff officers, who provided the link between the commander and his command by translating his decisions and wishes into detailed orders and transmitting them to the formations and units. Officers at different stages of their careers could serve as commanders or staff officers. A general might command an expeditionary force or serve as a senior staff officer at the War Office; a captain might command his company or act as his colonel's adjutant or as a junior staff officer in a higher headquarters. Efficient staff work was vital to success and, when so employed, an officer might achieve distinction; but he did not command, and it was the commander, at whatever level, who carried the responsibility for success or failure. Many officers considered in this book served in both functions, but it is as commanders that they are included.

Another rank matter must be mentioned as it will be encountered later. This was the brevet system, whereby regimental captains and upwards could be granted, usually for distinguished or meritorious conduct, a higher or 'brevet' rank in the Army while their regimental rank and pay remained unchanged. Thus a company captain, though junior in his regiment to other captains, might hold a brevet-majority/lieutenant-colonelcy in the Army, thus ultimately enhancing his chances of promotion to the higher ranks over the other, non-brevet-holding captains in his regiment.

---

1 Company regiments will be prefixed hereafter: HEIC, and Queen's regiments: HM.
2 At Plate A are three general officers in the full dress worn at different dates in the Victorian era.
3 These ranks changed, from 1876, to second-lieutenant.
4 Rudyard Kipling, The 'Eathen.

It should be remembered that until 1871 most promotion up to lieutenant-colonel was by purchase, except in the artillery, engineers and, before 1860, in the HEIC Armies, where seniority prevailed. Promotion above lieutenant-colonel was essentially a balance between seniority in the Army and merit.

Immediately prior to a campaign the designated units of horse, foot and guns would be grouped into fighting formations under their newly appointed senior commanders. Often neither the commanders nor the units had previous experience of working together, so had to learn their business as they went along. However, the Armies at home and abroad were relatively small; many of the officers, from largely similar backgrounds, were familiar with one another; and each individual unit, motivated by its regimental system and ethos and in healthy rivalry with the others, could usually be relied upon to implement successfully the overall commander's plan or redeem his errors. The Victorian military men, though perhaps less 'professional' than their modern counterparts, could usually extract some credit to themselves, their Queen and Empire even in defeat.

So, now to some of the commanders, of all ranks, who led the soldiers of the Queen. They will appear in sections divided into periods and theatres of operations wherein they became notable. Each section will be preceded by an outline of the operations it embraces.

INDIA 1837-56

Campaigns in Outline

As mentioned in the Introduction, this period began with the First Afghan War of 1838-42, an unsuccessful undertaking. Its reverses and retreats were somewhat avenged by Gen Pollock's Army of Retribution, but none of its commanders follow hereafter, although three who served in Afghanistan as junior ranks will be met later.

In 1839 the HEIC's invading army had traversed the independent and misgoverned territory of Sind. This had bred resentment and ultimately, in

HM 22nd Foot and Major Hutt's Bombay Artillery under attack during Sir Charles Napier's victory over the Baluchis at Meanee in Sind, 1843. Artist unknown.
(The Cheshire Regiment)

A Queen's infantry regiment charging the Sikhs at the battle of Gujerat where Sir Hugh Gough terminated the Second Sikh War, 1849. (Engraving from J.Grant, *British Battles on Land and Sea*)

1843, an attack on Sind's British Resident. The HEIC responded with a victorious punitive expedition – led by our first commander – and the annexation of Sind.

The next area of military operations was to the east, in the Maratha state of Gwalior, then in some internal disorder and with a powerful army posing a threat towards HEIC territory northwards. To forestall an invasion an HEIC force entered Gwalior and defeated the Marathas at Maharajpore and Punniar in what became known as 'the 48 Hours War'.

The next campaign occurred further north, in the Sikh domains of the Punjab which lay between the River Sutlej, then the western border of HEIC territory, and Afghanistan. The HEIC had maintained good relations with the Sikh ruler, Ranjit Singh, who had neither aided nor obstructed the HEIC invasion of Afghanistan in 1839. After his death internal struggles broke out from which the most powerful force to emerge was the Sikh army, the Khalsa. The Sikhs were a martial people with great fighting potential and the Khalsa had been trained by Europeans in modern methods, with a formidable artillery; it had formed a low opinion of the HEIC's native army during the Afghan War. In December 1845 the Khalsa crossed the Sutlej and invaded HEIC territory, thus starting the First Sikh War. It would last three months but proved so inconclusive that a second contest became inevitable. This was fought between November 1848 and March 1849, ending in British victory. The Punjab was annexed by the HEIC, whose boundary moved up to what became known as the North-West Frontier, adjoining Afghanistan and connecting with Sind to the south-west. In years to come the Punjab would provide some of the finest soldiers in the British service.

COMMANDERS

Charles Napier

The first memorable commander of this period, and of the Victorian era, is pictured in **Plate B**: the somewhat eccentric-looking conqueror of Sind, Major-General Sir Charles Napier, KCB[1], as he then was.

Born in 1782 into a noble, though not affluent Service family, he was the eldest of one naval and two military brothers. Before he was 18 he had served in four regiments, including the 95th Rifles at Sir John Moore's Shorncliffe Camp. As a major, aged 27, he commanded HM 50th Foot at Corunna, where he was wounded and captured. Having

1 A glossary of the abbreviations of British Orders will be found on page 2.

Sir Charles Napier in plain clothes, c.1840. Engraving from a photograph. (P.J.Haythornthwaite)

been exchanged, he returned to the Peninsula where he was again wounded, in the face. Recovering, he commanded HM 102nd Foot in America in 1813 before returning to the 50th.

During 1819-30 he administered part of the Ionian Islands, then under British protection, where he displayed great compassion towards the inhabitants, but intolerance of his superiors, who eventually dismissed him. Temporarily retired, he took up writing until reinstated in 1839 as a major-general and KCB, commanding England's Northern District, then in the grip of Chartism and civil unrest. By his sympathetic attitude to the Chartists he maintained law and order with minimum recourse to force of arms. Once the area was quiet he resigned.

In 1841, though nearly 60 and plagued by various painful ailments and his wounds, he accepted an HEIC post in Sind, chiefly to provide for his daughters by his late first wife, since he had no money but his pay. He expected trouble with the tyrannical Baluchi chiefs in Sind and, when they attacked the British Residency, he marched against them. With a mere 2,800 men, including only one Queen's regiment, HM 22nd Foot, he defeated 30,000 Baluchis at Meanee on 17 February 1843. A month later he beat them again, at Dubba (or Hyderabad), announcing his conquest with his famous Latin pun, *'Peccavi'* ('I have sinned'). It had been a masterly campaign, in difficult conditions and against huge odds. His subsequent restoration of order in Sind was marked by the same care for the ordinary folk and total ruthlessness to their oppressors that he had shown elsewhere. His period in command was yet again marred by arguments with his superiors, which eventually led to his return home in 1847.

Nevertheless, Napier was recalled to India in 1849 to replace Sir Hugh Gough (see below) following the latter's unsatisfactory handling of the Second Sikh War. However, Gough terminated the war before he could arrive. Napier became Commander-in-Chief, but soon further disagreements with the HEIC authorities forced him to resign in 1851. His wretched health deteriorated further, and two years later he died in Hampshire, aged 71, a lieutenant-general and GCB, beneath the Colours of HM 22nd which he had led in Sind and of which he was Colonel.

Whatever his differences with senior officers and officials, his courage and determination, his battles against enemies and with authority, and above all his humanity and consideration towards the less fortunate, all earned him the admiration of the public at large and especially of the ordinary soldiers. It was the latter who subscribed in greatest numbers towards his statue erected in Trafalgar Square.

With Napier in Plate B are two members of HEIC Bombay Army which, apart from HM 22nd Foot, provided most of his Sind force: a British officer of the Bombay Horse Artillery, and a Baluchi sowar of the Sind Irregular Horse.

Hugh Gough

In command during the Gwalior campaign and both Sikh Wars was General Sir Hugh (later Lord) Gough, GCB, who appears in **Plate C** with two of his subordinates after the battle of Sobraon, 10 February 1846.

Gough was born in 1779, fourth son to a colonel from a landed Irish family. He was commissioned ensign, aged 13, in his father's Limerick

Militia, becoming adjutant, aged 15, of the short-lived 119th Foot, and seeing his first action, aged 16, with HM 78th Highlanders at the capture of the Cape of Good Hope. He transferred to HM 87th, gaining a captaincy and his majority in its new 2nd Battalion. By 1809 he was commanding it, aged only 30, in the Peninsular War. He was wounded at Talavera but was still commanding at Barossa, where his men captured a French Eagle. He led the 2/87th up to 1813 when a bad hip wound forced him to go home. He was knighted in 1815.

In the post-war reductions the 2/87th was disbanded and Gough went on half-pay, living in Ireland, until returning to active duty just before he was promoted major-general in 1830. Despite his long military inactivity, his earlier reputation as an aggressive battalion commander earned him a divisional command in India in 1837. In 1841 he commanded, with great determination, the force sent from India for the First China War until the Chinese capitulated a year later.

Rewarded with a baronetcy, the GCB and the appointment of Commander-in-Chief, India, he was soon in action again with his rapid conquest of Gwalior. His attack at Maharajpore was watched by his wife, daughter and other ladies all mounted on elephants – which attracted heavy fire from the Maratha guns, although all survived undaunted.

Hugh Gough was a courageous general and a resolute if unsubtle tactician, with more faith in the bayonet than the musket or cannon ball. He encountered in the Sikh Khalsa his most dangerous opponent since the French of 30 years before. Always impetuous, he fought two battles at Mudki and Ferozeshah whose human cost and indecisive results caused the HEIC Governor-General to urge his recall. Before this could be effected a detached force won a victory at Aliwal, enabling Gough to prepare an assault on the Sikhs' main entrenched position at Sobraon.

Ignoring a sophisticated plan proposed by one of his staff, Gough ordered an artillery bombardment followed by a frontal attack. When the guns' ammunition was running out he uttered his famous, 'Thank God! I'll be at them with the bayonet!' By the stubborn courage of his Queen's regiments he won his victory, the war, and a barony – but again with severe loss, earning much criticism for his 'Tipperary tactics' and encouraging further attempts to secure his removal.

This animosity neither cost him the chief command then, nor caused him to change his methods, as became clear when he confronted the renewed Sikh threat in 1848. The casualties sustained in his frontal assault at Chillianwallah were so high, particularly in the leading Queen's regiments – HM 24th Foot losing half its strength – and the result so

The battle of Chillianwallah, Second Sikh War, Gough's most costly action. He can just be seen in the left centre of the picture on a white horse, in profile, wearing his white fighting coat. Lithograph by Dickenson after Capt.C.B.Young. (H.Cook, *The Sikh Wars*)

OPPOSITE **HM 16th Lancers charging Sikh infantry during Smith's masterly victory of Aliwal in the First Sikh War, 1846. After the battle Smith told the 16th: 'You have covered yourselves with glory'. Engraving after M.A.Hayes's watercolour. (FM E.Wood, VC, *British Battles on Land and Sea*)**

indecisive, that Sir Charles Napier was summoned (see above). However, Gough convincingly defeated the Sikhs at Gujerat and the war was won. After handing over the chief command to Napier he returned home.

For all his pugnacious and reckless obstinacy Gough won four campaigns and moreover the affection of his troops, despite the sacrifices he required of them. He received a viscountcy and other honours, became a field-marshal in 1862, and died in 1869 in his 90th year.

Harry Smith

Next in Plate C, with Gough, is Major-General Sir Harry Smith, KCB. Unlike several generals herein, whose early service encompassed numerous different regiments, Harry Smith, born in 1787 to a Cambridgeshire surgeon, never wore a red coat as a regimental officer – only the dark green of HM 95th Rifles, into which he was commissioned in 1805. With them he first saw action in South America in 1806, then throughout the Peninsular War, as a regimental and a staff officer in the famous Light Division from 1809 to 1814.

At the storming of Badajoz he met the Spanish girl, Juana de Leon, whom he married and who shared all his future fame. He had to leave her when he went to the American War but she accompanied him to Belgium for Waterloo, in which he was a brigade-major. Hearing that he had been killed, she made a harrowing search of the battlefield for his body until she met a friend who assured her that he was safe.

The next dozen years they spent in peacetime garrisons until he went to South Africa in 1828 as a staff colonel. In 1835 he made an epic ride of 600 miles in six days, from Cape Town to Grahamstown, to take command against Xhosa incursions on the Cape Frontier – the Sixth Kaffir, or Frontier War. His determined energy quelled the hostilities and earned him the governorship of the Frontier province, but disagreements with his superiors caused him to seek a transfer.

In 1840 he reached India as a major-general on the staff. He took the field with Gough, and with Juana, for the Gwalior campaign, both he and his wife nearly becoming casualties at Maharajpore, she with the elephant-borne

Harry Smith when a lieutenant-colonel in the Rifle Brigade (formerly 95th Rifles) shortly after Waterloo. After a portrait by Isabey. (P.J.Haythornthwaite)

Sir Harry Smith, aged 72 in 1859, as a full general and GCB. Engraving from a photograph. (J.Grant, *British Battles on Land and Sea*)

memsahibs (see above), he on the right flank when a roundshot nearly broke his leg and unhorsed him. Soon afterwards he was made KCB.

For the First Sikh War Gough gave him a division. At Mudki and Ferozeshah he led it very much from the front, especially when the Sikh resistance was fiercest, twice seizing a Colour of HM 50th to urge his men on and being the first man into the strongly-held village of Ferozeshah.

Three weeks later Gough detached him with a force to counter a Sikh threat to his communications. On 28 January, with 12,000 cavalry, infantry and artillery, Smith completely routed 16,000 Sikhs with 67 guns at Aliwal. Unlike Gough's reckless frontal assaults, Smith's victory demonstrated a perfectly co-ordinated use of all three arms, precisely timed, which earned him the Duke of Wellington's glowing praise in a speech at home. Rewarded with a GCB and a baronetcy, he rejoined Gough in time for Sobraon where, after several setbacks, his division attacked on the right and broke into the Sikh entrenchments in 'a brutal, bulldog fight'.

He and Juana went home to a hero's welcome. In 1847 they returned to South Africa where he became Governor of Cape Colony as a lieutenant-general. He oversaw the end of the Seventh Frontier War, but then faced a Boer rebellion which he defeated at Boomplaats in 1848. In 1850 began the Eighth and greatest Frontier War, which found Smith with a reduced garrison and growing friction with the Colonial Secretary over civil affairs. Wellington, as the Army's Commander-in-Chief, supported Smith's operations, but he could not prevent his replacement by Sir George Cathcart (see below). Although dismissed, Smith and his Juana left their mark on the Colony with the place-names of Ladysmith, Harrismith and Aliwal North.

He soldiered on in a few home commands, becoming a full general in 1854, and retiring at the age of 72 in 1859. He died the following year, his beloved and devoted Juana surviving him until 1872.

Bernard McCabe

Sgt McCabe raising HM 31st's Regimental Colour on the Sikh ramparts at the battle of Sobraon, 1846, the act which earned him his commission. Lithograph by J.Harris after H.Martens, from a sketch by Major G.White, HM 31st. (H.Cook, *The Sikh Wars*)

Plate C's third figure, depicted being presented by Smith to Gough, is another Irishman, Sergeant Bernard McCabe of HM 31st Foot. Enlisting in 1839, he served in the First Afghan War with Pollock's Army of Retribution in 1842. He fought in all the Sikh War battles and, at a critical moment in Smith's Sobraon attack, planted the 31st's Regimental Colour on the Sikh defences under heavy fire to encourage his men. He was one of several NCOs recommended by Gough for a commission, which he received in May 1846. He served as an ensign with HM 18th Foot in an 1847 China expedition, later exchanging into HM 32nd as a lieutenant, and fighting on the North-West Frontier in 1852. During the Mutiny the 32nd defended Lucknow, where McCabe proved himself a most gallant and tireless officer, being promoted captain in July 1857. Two months later he was mortally wounded while leading a sortie.

Unlike some ex-ranker officers, McCabe was greatly valued by all ranks of the 32nd and his brigadier, even earning the approval of his Colonel's lady. Had he survived, his work at Lucknow would have marked him for brevet promotion.

THE CRIMEAN WAR 1854-56

The War in Outline

With Queen Victoria on the throne, the last war British arms had fought against a European power had been with Imperial France and had culminated in Napoleon I's final defeat at Waterloo in 1815. Now, in the mid-19th century, the chief perceived threat from Europe was posed by Imperial Russia's ambitions in Asia and the consequent danger to British India, which led, as stated earlier, to the First Afghan War. In 1854 Britain, now in alliance with Napoleon III, declared war on Russia, ostensibly in support of the Ottoman Empire but in reality to deny Russia access to the Mediterranean from where she could duplicate her other threat to India from Central Asia.

The land fighting that followed occurred on the Crimean Peninsula before Sebastopol, base of the Russian Black Sea Fleet. To destroy this objective involved a landing; an advance punctuated by the successful battle of the Alma; the establishment of a base at Balaclava and siege lines around Sebastopol; another, chiefly cavalry, battle to defend Balaclava; the defeat of a major Russian counter-stroke at Inkerman; the enduring of a terrible winter in trenches, for which the British force was ill-prepared; and five months' siege operations until the Russians evacuated Sebastopol. Minor operations followed until peace was signed in March 1856. In sum, the war reflected little credit on the British Army's higher commanders and staff, but this was redeemed by the courage, endurance and tactical superiority over the Russians of the more junior commanders and their regiments.

COMMANDERS

Plate D depicts three Crimean commanders at different levels: regimental, brigade and division.

Lacy Yea

Lieutenant-Colonel Lacy Walter Yea commanded HM 7th Royal Fusiliers in the 1st Brigade of Lieutenant-General Sir George Brown's Light Division – a formation thought to contain some of the best-trained battalions in the Army, although its commander had seen no action since 1814.

The eldest son of a Somerset baronet and educated at Eton, Lacy Yea was aged 46 in 1854 and had been commanding the 7th for four years. Although a keen hunting man, his overriding preoccupation was his 'cherished regiment', as Kinglake called it. In peacetime, as a strict disciplinarian, he had been somewhat feared. In the Crimea his Fusiliers

soon realised that, in action, he was a fearless, strong-willed and most capable leader – 'the bravest of the brave', as Sergeant Gowing described him – and out of it, he would do all in his power to safeguard their welfare, particularly in the dreadful first winter.

At the Alma, on the extreme right of the Light Division's assault, he and his Fusiliers held their ground, alone and unsupported, against a superior Russian column's counter-attack, first protecting the Light Division's right flank as it was forced to retire, then guarding the 2nd Division's left as it advanced to support the Fusiliers.

The 7th were only partially committed at Inkerman. After preserving his regiment in better order than many during the winter, Yea was promoted to command the 1st Brigade of the Light Division in May 1855. In the ill-fated attack on the Redan on 18 June he led, from the front, the right-hand column against a decimating fire and was killed, sword in hand, at the Russian abattis. He was much mourned in the Crimean army and particularly by his Fusiliers.

James Scarlett

Enough has been written elsewhere about the battle of Balaclava and the performance and characters of the Cavalry Division and Light Brigade commanders, Lords Lucan and Cardigan; so next in Plate D is the Heavy Brigade commander, the Honourable Sir James Scarlett.

Born in 1799, second son of Baron Abinger, he was educated at Eton and Cambridge before joining the 18th Hussars as a cornet by purchase in 1818. He attained each subsequent rank by purchase, exchanging into the 5th Dragoon Guards in 1830 and as a lieutenant-colonel ten years later obtaining command of that regiment, which he exercised until the Crimean War.

Like his fellow cavalry commanders, he had seen no previous active or even Indian service but, unlike them, he was aware of his inexperience; when appointed to command the Heavy Brigade he selected for his staff two aides who had campaigned in India. He had done much to raise morale in his brigade, which included his own old regiment, during the army's disease-ridden stay at Varna. Consequently he enjoyed their confidence when action came at Balaclava. It was his

leading of the Heavies' uphill charge against superior numbers that achieved the cavalry's only unqualified success of that day.

Following Lucan's recall after Balaclava, Scarlett was promoted to major-general and command of the Cavalry Division, to the general approval of both brigades: 'a real old brick', wrote one officer. He remained in command until ill-health forced his return home in October 1855. Made KCB, he next commanded all cavalry at Aldershot, was Adjutant-General in Whitehall and, becoming lieutenant-general in 1862, commanded all troops at Aldershot from 1865 to 1870. He died in 1871, as GCB and Colonel of his old regiment.

Both Balaclava brigadiers were aristocratic cavalrymen unused to war; but the Heavies had the better man.

TOP **BrigGen Hon.James Scarlett at the head of the Heavy Brigade. Painting by Sir Francis Grant, PRA. (5th RI Dragoon Guards)**

ABOVE **The Heavy Brigade's charge at Balaclava, showing chiefly the Royal Scots Greys (2nd Dragoons), the centre regiment of Scarlett's first line. Painting by Felix Philoppoteaux. (Royal Scots Dragoon Guards)**

George Cathcart

Involved in the Light Brigade's disaster was the third figure of Plate D, the commander of the 4th Infantry Division, Lieutenant-General the Honourable Sir George Cathcart, KCB. Aged 60, he was nevertheless one of the two youngest of the divisional commanders and the only one with recent experience of an operational command. In 1852 he had relieved Sir Harry Smith (see above) as Governor of Cape Colony and commander of all British forces in the Eighth Frontier War, which he terminated in 1853.

His military life had begun at the age of 16 in 1810 as a cornet in the 2nd Life Guards, the first of four cavalry and four infantry regiments in which he had held ranks, all by purchase, including HM 8th Foot and the King's Dragoon Guards, both of which he commanded. His early years of commissioned service had been spent not at regimental duty but as an ADC: first to his father the Earl Cathcart, then Ambassador to the Russian

Tsar, in which capacity he observed much fighting during Napoleon's 1812 invasion of Russia, and secondly on Wellington's staff at Waterloo.

After returning from South Africa in 1854 he was briefly Adjutant-General in Whitehall before being given the 4th Division for the Crimea. Cathcart's recent campaigning experience also earned him a secret 'dormant' commission, whereby he would take over the army if anything befell Lord Raglan (see below), despite not being the next senior general.

Yet he and his division were denied any significant part in the attack at the Alma. Touchy and irritable as he was by nature, and now holding a subordinate appointment rather than the chief command as in South Africa, he did not take kindly to his division being left out of the war's first battle.

When the Russian threat developed against Balaclava

TOP **Hon.Sir George Cathcart with his staff and escort of 12th Lancers in South Africa, 1852. Lithograph after a painting by Capt Goodrich, Cape Mounted Rifles. In the original painting Cathcart's long boots are depicted higher, as in Plate D3. (Africana Museum)**

ABOVE **Gen Cathcart's death in the valley below the Kitspur during his ill-conceived counter-attack against orders at the battle of Inkerman, 5 November 1854. (P.J.Mercer)**

– defended only by the Cavalry Division and HM 93rd Highlanders – Cathcart was ordered to march his division down from the siege lines. Not only did he waste 40 minutes before starting; he did nothing to hurry his division's march, made no attempt to concert a plan with Lucan, and only moved forward in support of the cavalry after the Light Brigade had been destroyed.

At Inkerman his tendency always to know best led him to disobey Raglan's orders, to ignore the 1st Division's request for help, and to attack down a ravine where he became cut off and overwhelmed. 'I fear we are in a scrape', he said, whereupon he was killed.

Difficult and opinionated as he may have been with his peers, he was nevertheless generally liked and respected by the junior ranks. He welcomed the 1st Rifle Brigade, which had served under him in South Africa, to the 4th Division with a personal gift to every Rifleman of a waterproof sheet, a useful article not issued to other troops. Cathcart was a gifted, experienced officer with many advantages, yet he ultimately destroyed his reputation and himself.

Fitzroy Somerset, Lord Raglan

After these subordinate commanders, we depict at **Plate E** the Commander-in-Chief of the Crimean army himself, General (later Field-Marshal) Lord Raglan, GCB, shown with two subordinates at the greatest battle of the war, Inkerman, on 5 November 1854.

Born in 1788 as Lord Fitzroy Somerset, 13th child of the 5th Duke of Beaufort, he served in the Army for 51 of his 67 years, yet only actually commanded any body of troops in war in the last two years of his life. Nevertheless that command was against the major European power of the age, rather than the Asiatic or African enemies (however formidable) faced by other more battle-experienced officers herein, and he consequently deserves a place among them.

After a brief education at Westminster he received a cornetcy in the 4th Light Dragoons just before his 16th birthday. Four years later he was a captain, though with little soldiering to show for it, only attachment as an aide on a diplomatic mission to Turkey. Then came his next appointment, as ADC to the Duke of Wellington (then still Wellesley) when he began his command in the Peninsular War in 1808.

So began a military association and close friendship which were to last for 44 years. Somerset held different ranks in four regiments but never served with them. He was involved in more diplomatic missions, but mostly, as he rose from captain to major-general, he served as Wellington's Military Secretary. As such he witnessed 15 battles in the Peninsula, being wounded at Busaco and losing his right arm at Waterloo, but earning the KCB. After 1815 he continued at Wellington's side during the Duke's appointments as Master-General of the Ordnance (MGO) and Commander-in-Chief of the Army. As the Duke aged more work fell upon Somerset which he loyally performed for his old chief. When Wellington died in 1852

Raglan, then Lord Fitzroy Somerset, as Military Secretary to the Duke of Wellington at the battle of Salamanca, 1812. Detail from painting by Richard Hook for Men-at-Arms 84, *Wellington's Generals*. (Osprey Publishing)

Lord Raglan presiding at an Allied Council of War in his Crimean headquarters during the siege of Sebastopol. Print from a drawing by William Simpson. (Author's collection)

Raglan in full dress as a major-general, KCB, in c.1845. Engraving. (J.Grant, *British Battles on Land and Sea*)

Somerset had hoped to succeed him as C-in-C, but had to be content with Wellington's earlier post of MGO, a peerage as 1st Baron Raglan and the GCB. While acting (very capably) as MGO, he was appointed to command the Army of the East on the outbreak of war with Russia.

Although he had closely observed Wellington exercising command in the field between 1808 and 1815, he had never commanded so much as a company himself. He had shown courage and ability as a staff officer on the battlefield, but he had spent the last 39 years in a Whitehall office. Inevitably, too, he had become much influenced by Wellington's conservatism about the Army. Seniority was obviously a factor in selection for this important command and, of four possible contenders of sufficient seniority (one being Gough – see above), Raglan, at 66, was the only one then aged under 70.

He was kindly, courteous and conscientious, but not a natural commander. The victories of Alma and Inkerman and the avoidance of defeat at Balaclava were secured by his troops, not by his tactical skill and leadership. The dreadful sufferings of those troops in the first winter, and his inability to respond, elicited much criticism of him, both from the army and from those at home. When the June assault on Sebastopol failed he died, as much from depression and the burden of command as from failing health. He was much mourned in the army, even by his critics. Florence Nightingale summed him up: 'He was not a very good general, but he was a very good man'.

John Pennefather

Raglan was present, but made only one tactical decision, at Inkerman, a battle which was won by the gunners' and infantrymen's outstanding conduct under the untiring leadership of the next figure in Plate E, Major-General John Lysaght Pennefather.

The son of a Tipperary parson, he was commissioned cornet in 1818 in the 7th Dragoon Guards, but exchanged into HM 22nd Foot as a captain in 1826, and commanded it for ten years from 1839. His 22nd was the only Queen's regiment engaged in Napier's conquest of Sind (see above), and had a leading role at Meanee where Pennefather, temporarily commanding its brigade, was badly wounded but was made CB.

LtCol John Pennefather, then commanding HM 22nd Foot, lying wounded (left foreground) on the battlefield of Meanee, 1843 (see under Charles Napier). Detail of a painting by George Jones. (The Cheshire Regiment)

MajGen John Pennefather (left) in 1855 when commanding the 2nd Division in the Crimea, with a 4th Light Dragoons orderly. Photograph by Roger Fenton. (R.G.Harris)

He was promoted major-general in June 1854 and took command of the 1st Brigade of General de Lacy Evans' 2nd Division for the Crimea. This division attacked on the right at the Alma and later, after the siege lines had been established before Sebastopol, was given the important responsibility of guarding those lines' right rear.

It was in this area that the Russians made their exploratory attack on 26 October and their main effort on 5 November. By then the cheery and combative Pennefather was popular with all ranks of his brigade, to whom he was known as 'Old Blood and Ounds' from one of his many and colourful expletives. In the first action, known as 'Little Inkerman', Pennefather handled his brigade well in accordance with Evans' successful battle plan. By 5 November Evans was unwell, so Pennefather led and inspired the whole 2nd Division, and the reinforcements that later appeared, in an epic resistance against the massive Russian onslaught. Towards the end, judging correctly the right time for a counter-attack, he told Raglan and the French Gen Canrobert that, given reinforcements, he would 'lick them to the devil'. His spirited assertion inspired the Frenchman to pronounce him *'Quel bon général'*, but he nevertheless declined to commit his troops. Even so Pennefather could justifiably claim that he and his men had given the Russians 'a hell of a towelling'. He retained command of the 2nd Division until invalided home in July 1855.

After the war he commanded the Aldershot District as a lieutenant-general and KCB, was promoted general in 1868, and died in post as Governor of the Royal Hospital, Chelsea, a popular figure among its Pensioners.

Frederick Haines

The third figure on Plate E also had a vital, if more subordinate role at Inkerman: Captain (Brevet Lieutenant-Colonel) Frederick Paul Haines, HM 21st Royal North British Fusiliers.

Born in 1820 into a military family from Sussex, he was commissioned ensign in 1839 into HM 4th Foot, then in India, and lieutenant a year later. In that rank he was appointed Military Secretary to Sir Hugh Gough (see above) for the First Sikh War. He was present at Mudki and was badly wounded at Ferozeshah by grapeshot, having his horse killed under him. He was promoted captain, without purchase, in HM 10th Foot but continued on Gough's staff throughout the battles of the Second Sikh War. His services were rewarded with a brevet lieutenant-colonelcy but, having exchanged into HM 21st RNB Fusiliers, he was still a captain regimentally when he reached the Crimea with them in Cathcart's 4th Division (see above).

Gen Sir Frederick Haines, GCB, GCSI, CIE, in later life when Commander-in-Chief of the Army in India 1876-81. Engraving from a photograph. (J.Grant, *Recent British Battles on Land and Sea*)

Haines and the right wing of HM 21st Royal North British Fusiliers defending the Barrier at the battle of Inkerman. Painting by Marjorie Wetherstone. (Royal Highland Fusiliers)

At Inkerman the 21st was one of the regiments that reinforced Pennefather's hard-pressed 2nd Division. Half was sent to the left; the remainder, including Haines' company, under Lieutenant-Colonel Ainslie with HM 63rd, successfully charged a Russian column. Haines ended this charge at a stone wall blocking a road leading into the British position called the Barrier, with two more Russian columns beyond him. Ainslie being killed, Haines took command of the remaining Fusiliers and small parties from other regiments at the Barrier. He held this position against repeated attacks for six hours. Eventually, spotting an opportunity and asking Pennefather for reinforcements (which could not be spared), he launched part of his small force against the Russian gunners who immediately withdrew, and so began the whole Russian retreat.

Haines served with the 21st for the rest of the war but never acceded to its command through lack of seniority. In 1859, however, when acting as Military Secretary to the C-in-C Madras, he was appointed lieutenant-colonel in HM 8th Foot. He commanded its 1st Battalion at home until 1861 when he was given a brigade at Aldershot.

Promoted major-general in 1864, he held two senior commands in Madras between 1869 and 1875, punctuated by a year as Quartermaster-General at the War Office in 1870. Finally he was appointed to the prestigious post of Commander-in-Chief India in 1876-81, during which he held overall responsibility for the Second Afghan War (see below), when his sound military judgements caused friction with the head-strong Viceroy, Lord Lytton, who resigned. Haines received the GCB, GCSI and CIE and in 1890 he was promoted field-marshal. He died in 1910, aged 90.

In later life, notwithstanding all his distinctions, he always looked back on his defence of the Barrier as the highlight of his career, saying 'It was worth living to have been at Inkerman'.

HM 52nd Light Infantry of Nicholson's column storming the Kashmir Gate at the assault on Delhi, 14 September 1857. (P.J.Haythornthwaite)

INDIA 1857-98

This period falls into two sections: the Indian Mutiny 1857-59, and the post-Mutiny reorganisation with accompanying campaigns.

The Mutiny in Outline

The Indian Mutiny was the second of the three chief wars of the Victorian epoch. Although the Crimea was a European war, the Mutiny lasted longer; its land operations covered a wider area,

and required greater forces. Lord Roberts (see below) called it 'that calamitous crisis of our rule in India'. It has been covered in other works published by Osprey, in which its causes, events and rival forces can be found in more detail[1]. Suffice it to say here that it involved the near-total revolt of the HEIC's largest army, of Bengal, to which various disaffected elements attached themselves. Against them were ranged the Queen's troops in or sent to India, the HEIC's European regiments, its Madras and Bombay Armies[2], the Punjab Irregular Force, and many of the northern races who enlisted in new regiments.

The fighting fell into three major campaigns: the operations to recapture Delhi, May-September 1857; those centred on Cawnpore, Lucknow and Oudh, June 1857-May 1858; and Central India (Jhansi, Rajputana, Gwalior), June 1857-June 1858. Mopping-up operations continued until April 1859.

John Nicholson, aged 29, while on his first and last home leave in 1850-51 before becoming Deputy Commissioner of Bannu Province on the North-West Frontier. (Dr M.Bruce)

MUTINY COMMANDERS

There were some serious command failures at the start of the Mutiny. Those who follow, and are depicted in **Plate F**, helped to avert the threatened calamity: three very different individuals, yet with some formative influences in common.

John Nicholson

Nicholson, shown here as a brigadier-general at Delhi, was an HEIC officer who spent 11 of 18 years' commissioned service as an administrator or staff officer – yet his contemporaries thought him an outstanding commander.

An Ulsterman, born the son of a doctor in 1822 under rather reduced circumstances, he received an HEIC cadetship through an uncle's gift. He went to the First Afghan War with HEIC 27th Bengal Native Infantry but was captured and held prisoner for six months. After serving with the commissariat in the First Sikh War, his career as a political officer in Kashmir and the Punjab began through a previous meeting with Sir Henry Lawrence, who had spotted his potential. With the Sikhs again troublesome in 1848, Nicholson scoured the country with some Pathan levies to acquire intelligence and quell disorder. When war recommenced he served Gough as a commisariat/political/intelligence officer, no task daunting him. Promoted captain in 1848, he received a brevet-majority for his war service.

With the Punjab annexed, he became responsible for Bannu on the NW Frontier, a hotbed of dissidence. Of imposing appearance, with stern principles stiffened by daily Bible-reading, he ruled his district energetically, with humanity for the weak but ruthlessness for malefactors. Such was his prestige among the hard-bitten tribesmen that he was worshipped by some as a god – 'Nikalseyn'.

When the Mutiny erupted in May 1857 he was Deputy Commissioner at Peshawar, headquarters of the NW Frontier District. Quickly appreciating how vital was the security of the recently-conquered Punjab and the adjoining Frontier, he and his chief Herbert Edwardes formed a moveable column and enlisted local levies to hunt down mutineers, disarm doubtful units and eradicate sedition. Nicholson rode tirelessly for miles with his ever-loyal Multani Horse. Edwardes later wrote: 'I never saw another like him, so undaunted, so heroic, yet so modest.'

By mid-June the region was sufficiently secure for the Moveable Column's transfer to bolster the force besieging Delhi. In command was Nicholson, now brigadier-general aged 34. During his 500-mile march he disarmed or destroyed large bodies of mutineers. Despite his lack of command experience, he brought a fresh mind and unyielding determination to the lacklustre siege operations. Soon after reaching Delhi on 14 August he led out a 2,000-strong force to attack some 7,000 mutineers attempting to intercept the approach of the British siege-train. This victory at Najafgarh earned Nicholson the Governor-General's assessment that he was 'a born general'.

Though often at odds with his seniors and elders, his arrival reinvigorated the Delhi Field Force. His forceful activity and perceptive appreciations of the situation largely determined the decision to assault on 14 September. While personally leading the column which had forced the Kashmir Gate he was mortally wounded within the city. He died on 22 September; his funeral was attended, against their colonel's orders, by all soldiers of HM 52nd which had come with him from Peshawar and stormed the Kashmir Gate. Lord Roberts, who as a subaltern knew him well, remembered him as 'the *beau ideal* of a soldier and a gentleman'.

Statue of John Nicholson at the Royal School, Dungannon, Co.Tyrone, where he was educated 1834-38. Another statue of him stands in Lisburn, Co.Antrim, where he was born. (A.Higgins)

Henry Havelock

Major-General Sir Henry Havelock, KCB, was, like Nicholson, a man of profound religious beliefs. He hailed from a once-rich family which fell upon hard times, thereby altering his planned legal career to a military one, but with very slow promotion prospects due to lack of finance.

Born in 1795, he had begun legal training when his shipbuilder father lost his fortune. He obtained a commission in HM 95th Rifles in 1815, first serving at home in Harry Smith's (see above) company, but transferring to HM 13th Foot in 1822 to serve in India.

Once there he spent more of his free time with missionaries than at race-meetings, or with a group he assembled of teetotal, Bible-reading soldiers known as 'Havelock's Saints', or simply studying his profession. His studies paid off, and in the First Burma War of 1825 he was appointed to the force commander's staff though still only a subaltern. His staff experience and a long period

The second relief of Lucknow, 17 November 1857. Havelock, with Sir James Outram beside him, greets Sir Colin Campbell; behind the white horse's head is Sir Hope Grant, mounted. Detail after the painting by T.J.Barker. (FM E.Wood, VC, *British Battles on Land and Sea*)

OPPOSITE **Henry Havelock in general officer's full dress tunic, c.1857. Engraving after a portrait by C.Holl.** (P.J.Haythornthwaite)

as adjutant of the 13th eventually earned him promotion to captain after 23 years as a subaltern – and being passed over by 'three sots and two fools' – in time for the First Afghan War. He served both on the staff and with the 13th, particularly during its five-month defence of Jellalabad in 1841-42. He was prominent in all the operations and was rewarded with a brevet-majority and the CB.

In 1843, now aged 48, he at last became a major, without purchase. He joined Gough's staff for the Gwalior campaign and subsequently for both Sikh Wars. Staff work involved much hard riding under fire on the battlefield, and Havelock had horses shot under him three times by the Sikhs. In 1849 he was invalided home after 26 years in India, but returned to take up a senior staff post at army headquarters in 1854 as a lieutenant-colonel with a brevet-colonelcy.

In 1857 he received his first major command, of the 2nd Division in Sir James Outram's expeditionary force to Persia. He missed the early engagements but it was his plan, submitted to Outram, that effected the capture of Mohammerah and largely terminated the war.

By the time he returned to India the Mutiny had begun. Now aged 62 and a brigadier-general, he was given a column assembled at Allahabad of only four under-strength battalions, all just returned from Persia, with a handful of irregular cavalry and six guns, for the recapture of Cawnpore – whose garrison had just been butchered after surrendering – and the relief of Lucknow's embattled defenders (mostly HM 32nd – see McCabe above). Havelock began the 126-mile advance on 7 July, making forced marches in the hottest month of the Indian summer; he fought three successful actions, and finally routed the Nana Sahib's 5,000 men outside Cawnpore on the 16th, but was too late to save the garrison's women and children from massacre – as revealed by the horrific sights his soldiers encountered.

It took his small force two months to reach Lucknow, his first attempt having failed due to stronger opposition, cholera, and logistic difficulties. Once reinforced after returning to Cawnpore, he tried again. It took a battle en route and two days of fierce fighting to break into Lucknow, but late on 25 September Havelock reached the Residency's still undefeated garrison. However, with the enemy still in strength around the city, his relief column had become merely a reinforcement. There followed another seven weeks of siege before Sir Colin Campbell achieved the second relief (see below) on 16 November. Eight days later Havelock died of dysentery just after learning he had been made KCB, but unaware of his baronetcy and promotion to major-general.

Gen Sir James Hope Grant, GCB, c.1870. Engraving from a photograph. (J.Grant, *British Battles on Land and Sea*)

His last words to his VC son, long his aide-de-camp, were 'See how a Christian can die'. To the British public, this devout little general, still dedicated after long years of slow advancement, became a national hero.

Hope Grant

Major-General Sir James Hope Grant, KCB, was the unusual combination of a dashing cavalryman and an accomplished cellist, and – like Nicholson and Havelock – a committed Christian. Born in 1808, he was commissioned cornet in HM 9th Lancers in 1826, and rose by purchase to captain in 1835. He remained with that one regiment (unlike many other officers described here) until he was promoted major-general in 1858.

He filled a staff post in the First China War as brigade-major to Lord Saltoun, who brought up reinforcements for Gough's army in 1842. Saltoun – a hero of Hougoumont in 1815 – had selected Grant for both his military and musical abilities, he himself being a keen violinist. Created CB for his services and promoted major, without purchase, Grant returned to his regiment in India, serving at the battle of Sobraon in 1845. He commanded the 9th Lancers through the Second Sikh War, gaining his lieutenant-colonelcy, again without purchase, which was unusual for a cavalry officer.

Grant won the respect and popularity of all ranks in the 9th, which remained in India until the Mutiny. They marched from Ambala in May 1857 to join the Delhi Field Force where, with the Carabiniers, they formed a cavalry brigade under Grant's command, reinforced later by loyal regiments from the Punjab. During the three-month siege this brigade fought several successful actions against enemy sorties, always led by Grant, who was on one occasion unhorsed and nearly captured.

After the fall of Delhi Grant led a column (accompanied by his cello on a camel …) to reinforce Sir Colin Campbell for the second relief of Lucknow. At the third battle of Cawnpore soon afterwards he mounted a masterly attack of cavalry and horse artillery on enemy squares. Promoted major-general in February 1858, he continued to command the cavalry, now a division strong, at Campbell's final capture of Lucknow in March and during the subsequent fighting in Oudh and Rohilkand. His Mutiny services raised him to KCB; those of his old 9th Lancers earned them no fewer than 14 Victoria Crosses.

Grant's reputation soon brought him promotion to lieutenant-general and an independent command: of the force sent from India for the Third China War of 1860 in conjunction with the French. Although these allies proved less than co-operative, in three months Grant captured the

LtCol Hope Grant's regiment, HM 9th Lancers, surprising mutineers outside Delhi during the siege. Lithograph after Capt G.F.Atkinson. (Staff College)

Taku Forts, defeated the Chinese three times in the open en route to Peking, and captured the city. Grant distributed his share of the Summer Palace's booty among his men. His first-rate handling of the campaign, tactically and logistically, won him the GCB and the admiration of the Queen, the British public and all his troops.

Returning to India he commanded the Madras Army in 1862-63, then went home to become Quartermaster-General. In 1870, aged 62, he took over the chief command at Aldershot where, against opposition, he revised the training methods, started annual autumn manoeuvres and wargames, devised an improved system of cavalry outpost duties based on his Mutiny experiences, and did much for his soldiers' welfare. One of his staff officers whose career he encouraged, and whom he had encountered in the Mutiny and China, will be met later – Garnet Wolseley. However, years of foreign service had taken their toll on Grant's health and he died in 1875. Sir John Fortescue wrote of him: 'Not many men have better understood war than this kindly, pious, daring lancer who could play as skilfully on the hearts of his men as on the strings of his beloved violincello'.

Colin Campbell

At **Plate G** is one of the major Mutiny commanders, Lieutenant-General Sir Colin Campbell, GCB, Commander-in-Chief India from August 1857, depicted with two lower ranks just before the storming of the Secunderbagh during the second relief of Lucknow on 16 November 1857.

MajGen Sir Colin Campbell at the time of the Crimean War. Engraving from a photograph. (P.J.Haythornthwaite)

Not only did Campbell have a distinguished record of field service, but he was a man of humble origins who achieved the highest rank and a peerage. Born in 1792, son of a Glaswegian carpenter named Macliver, he acquired the name of Campbell and an ensigncy in HM 9th Foot in 1808 through his maternal uncle's interest. Though then aged only 16, he was to display great courage, endurance and leadership as a company subaltern throughout the entire Peninsular War. He especially distinguished himself at San Sebastian where, despite recovering from a double wound, he volunteered to lead the 'forlorn hope', only to be wounded again at the breach. Discharging himself from hospital though still very lame, he caught up with the 9th in time for the crossing of the Bidassoa, where yet another wound forced his return home. His service was rewarded with a captaincy without purchase, but his wounds and a fever contracted during the 1809 Walcheren expedition were to affect his health thereafter.

He devoted much of his time during the post-war years, while serving at home and abroad with various regiments, to a serious study of his profession. In 1835, with financial help from friends, he obtained command of HM 98th Foot which he led with distinction in the 1842 China

War. Posted to India, he served as a brigade and divisional commander in the Second Sikh War, sustaining another wound at Ramnuggar, leading the pursuit of the defeated Sikhs after Gujerat, and being made KCB in 1849. Afterwards he conducted some of the earliest expeditions on the NW Frontier in 1851-52.

The carpenter's son was now Sir Colin and a major-general. For the Crimea he was given the Highland Brigade (HM 42nd, 79th and 93rd). His leadership and popularity with his Highlanders, together with his tactical perception, led to his decisive rout of the Russian right at the Alma. Made responsible for Balaclava harbour's security, he held it against the Russian cavalry with the 93rd's 'thin red line', exhorting them to 'Remember there is no retreat from here. You must die where you stand'. After Inkerman he replaced the Duke of Cambridge as commander of the 1st Division. A year later, after Raglan's successor Simpson resigned, Campbell was a contender for the chief command, but was passed over in favour of a more junior and less-experienced general; this he resented, but later he was made GCB and granted an audience with the Queen.

When offered the chief command in India during the Mutiny, he sailed within 24 hours. On arrival he saw his first task as the second relief of Lucknow (see Havelock) but realised that much logistic preparation was first necessary. The inevitable delay earned him the misnomer 'Sir Crawling Camel', but his thorough planning, forceful character and ruthlessness with incompetence paved the way to the successful relief and evacuation of the Lucknow garrison in November – with his favourite 93rd Highlanders much in evidence – followed by a victory over Tantia Tope outside Cawnpore in December.

Lucknow had been re-occupied by the mutineers, whom Campbell attacked and routed in March 1858. He then set about clearing Oudh and Rohilkand until rebel activity ceased.

Created Baron Clyde and KSI for his services, he retained the Indian command until 1860 when ill-health sent him home. He was promoted field-marshal and died, much honoured and beloved, in 1863. He was buried in Westminster Abbey.

Exemplifying Campbell's empathy with soldiers is the central figure in Plate G, representing Sergeant Joe Lee, a Welshman of HM 53rd always known as 'Dobbin', who had served under Campbell in the Punjab ten years earlier. Just before the Secunderbagh assault, when its walls had been breached, Lee called out to Campbell 'Sir Colin, let the two "Thirds" at them!' (meaning the 53rd and 93rd). Campbell, who seldom forgot a face, inquired 'Isn't that Sergeant Dobbin?' Assured that it was, he asked Lee if the breach was wide enough. Lee thought it could be forced, so Campbell ordered the Punjabis forward. Later in life Lee remained in India after his service ended, becoming manager of the Railway Hotel, Cawnpore, where he was recognised in 1892 by a former 93rd Highlander.

John Ewart

Facing Campbell in Plate G is Major (Brevet Lieutenant-Colonel) John Alexander Ewart, HM 93rd Highlanders. Born in 1821 into a Scottish military family and graduating from the Royal Military College, Sandhurst, in 1838, Ewart spent his early commissioned service in an English regiment, HM 35th Foot. He exchanged into the 93rd as a

captain in 1846, receiving a brevet majority just before that regiment landed in the Crimea as part of Campbell's Highland Brigade. He commanded a company at the Alma and again in the 93rd's famous action at Balaclava, although by then he was officially on Raglan's staff. In that capacity he brought the first warning of the Russian attack at Inkerman to Raglan. Promoted major, he rejoined the 93rd in February 1855 for the rest of the war, receiving his next brevet in November.

This rank he still held when the 93rd arrived in India as part of the Mutiny reinforcements, to be brigaded with HM 53rd Foot and HEIC 4th Punjabis for Campbell's second relief of Lucknow. In the attack on the Secunderbagh on 16 November Ewart commanded the 93rd's seven assault companies in support of the Punjabis. When the latter's attack wavered Campbell ordered Ewart, 'Bring on the tartan! Let my own lads at them!' The Highlanders surged over the wall and, in fierce hand-to-hand fighting with Ewart leading, cleared the courtyard and buildings as the Punjabis followed and the 53rd got in on the right. Ewart fought two enemy officers to seize a Colour, despite a wound to his sword arm. When resistance ceased he presented his trophy to Campbell, who rebuked him for leaving his men, but later apologised. Just before the Cawnpore battle in December Ewart lost his left arm from a cannon shot while inspecting the picquets. He was much missed in the 93rd. For his Mutiny service he was made CB, ADC to the Queen and promoted.

Blocked from commanding the 93rd by its colonel remaining in post until 1860, Ewart exchanged into the 78th Highlanders, commanding them from 1859 to 1864. He was, however, Honorary Colonel of his old regiment from 1895 until he died in 1904. By then he had risen to full general and KCB, becoming a GCB two days before his death.

Gen Sir John Ewart, KCB, in later life, c.1895, as Colonel of the Argyll and Sutherland Highlanders (91st and 93rd). Note his empty left sleeve. (P.J.Haythornthwaite)

Post-Mutiny Reorganisation & Campaigns, 1860-98

After the Mutiny the East India Company was dissolved and sovereignty of British India became vested in the Queen who ruled through the Governor-General or Viceroy. He answered to the British Government's Secretary of State for India, head of the India Office in London. In 1877 the Queen was declared Empress of India.

The Army in India was much changed. The three Presidency armies and the Punjab Frontier Force (PFF) were retained but forming one Indian Army. The Bengal Army was refashioned with new regiments, its men now being drawn primarily from the 'martial races' of the north-west, especially the Punjab. In 1895 the three armies and the PFF were reorganised into four Commands. The pre-Mutiny proportion of British troops to Indian of 1:9 was increased so that, by 1863, there were 62,000 British to 125,000 Indian. All artillery henceforth was British-manned except for the PFF's mountain artillery. The HEIC's European units, of all arms, were incorporated into the British Army.

Until 1895 the PFF came under the Punjab's Lieutenant Governor and outside the jurisdiction of the Commander-in-Chief India. The latter was also C-in-C Bengal, and had some general control over the Cs-in-C of Madras and Bombay.

From 1860 the reorganised Indian Army plus British regiments stationed in India (i.e. the Army in India) was operationally employed chiefly on the NW Frontier. Here the next 40 years saw 28 expeditions of varying size and duration (apart from ten to the North-East), culminating in the largest of all, the Great Pathan Revolt of 1897-98. In addition the continuing perceived Russian threat led to the Second Afghan War, 1878-1880. The Army in India's services were also required in China (1859-60), Burma (1885-92), Malaya (1875) and westwards to Abyssinia (1868), Malta (1878), Egypt (1882) and Sudan (1885). Three of the four latter will feature in the Africa section following.

Cavalry, infantry and mountain artillery types of the Punjab Frontier Force, c.1890, whose regiments were most frequently engaged on the NW Frontier. The Guides Cavalry and Infantry (left) were the first British or Indian regiment to adopt khaki clothing, from 1846. Print after R.Simkin. (Author's collection)

POST-MUTINY COMMANDERS

In contrast to the more senior officers considered above, **Plate H** features three of the Army in India's junior commanders, at company level, who achieved fame respectively in the 1860 China War, in Afghanistan, and on the Frontier.

Robert Rogers

Leading the assault on the Taku Forts on 21 August 1860 (see Hope Grant above) were HM 44th and 67th Regiments. Foremost among the 44th was Lieutenant Robert Montresor Rogers, who won the Victoria Cross for giving a lead to his men by first swimming a defensive ditch in front of the walls under heavy fire, then clambering up an embrasure to be first into the fort. He was closely followed by Private McDougall of his regiment and Lieutenant Lenon, 67th, who also won VCs.

A cigarette card commemorating the Victoria Crosses won by Lt R.M.Rogers, HM 44th Regiment (top) and Lt E.H.Lenon, HM 67th (below) at the storming of the Taku Forts, Third China War, 1860. (Author's collection)

Rogers, born in Dublin in 1834 and gazetted ensign in the 44th in 1855, and lieutenant six months later, both without purchase, had fought in the Crimea in the final Sebastopol operations. He went with the 44th to India during the Mutiny but, being stationed in Madras, saw no action. Returning to India from China, he was promoted captain, again without purchase, and exchanged into HM 90th Light Infantry. He served with the 90th in India, at home and in the Ninth Frontier War in 1878, rising to command the regiment throughout the Zulu War, notably at Kambula and Ulundi, receiving a brevet-colonelcy. He left the 90th in 1882, later commanded a brigade in India, and retired as a major-general and CB in 1889. He died in Berkshire in 1895.

Walter Hamilton

The nature of the terrain and type of fighting on the NW Frontier and in Afghanistan demanded junior officers of high calibre, who often found themselves separated from the close supervision and support of their superiors. This was particularly so in Indian Army units, where subalterns often received greater responsibility earlier than their British Army counterparts. The most seasoned Frontier regiment was the Corps of Guides, recruited from the pick of the 'martial races', whose young officers learned their trade from many notable seniors, like the three famous Battye brothers who were all killed in action.

One of Wigram Battye's subalterns in the Guides Cavalry was Lieutenant Walter Richard Pollock Hamilton. Born in 1856 into a well-connected Irish family and educated at Felstead, he was originally commissioned into HM 70th Regiment, which he joined in India in 1874. Hamilton was tall, handsome, a bold horseman and polo-player, with a quick wit, a gift for languages and a taste for poetry. While still with the 70th at Rawalpindi he met Wigram Battye, who noted his potential. On promotion to lieutenant Hamilton was offered and accepted a transfer to the Guides.

He first saw Frontier action with them against the Jowaki Afridis in 1877-78, also acting as ADC to the expedition commander, and immediately afterwards against the Utman Khel and Ranizais. He was thus experienced when the Second Afghan War began in late 1878.

The Guides advanced up the Khyber Pass with Gen Sir Sam Browne's force to Jellalabad. They saw some skirmishing, but no major action until March 1879 when 5,000 hostile tribesmen were encountered near Futtehabad by an all-arms column including 200 Guides Cavalry under Wigram Battye with Hamilton as his only British subaltern. When the horse artillery ceased fire to change position the tribesmen advanced rapidly. Despite the odds Battye ordered the charge. Leading from the front, he was twice hit, unhorsed, and just before he was hit again, mortally, he shouted to Hamilton, 'Take them on, Wally!' Hamilton took the lead, closely followed by his sowars eager to avenge their beloved commander and, after fierce close-quarter fighting, routed the enemy. During the charge Hamilton rushed to the aid of a dismounted trooper, killed the three men attacking him and saved his life. He was later recommended for the VC, but never learned of the award.

In July 1879, though only 23, he was selected to command the 78-strong Guides detachment forming the escort to Sir Louis Cavagnari's mission to Kabul. On 3 September the British Residency was attacked by a huge mob

of Afghan soldiery. From 8.45 in the morning Hamilton and his Guides defended the Residency. In mid-afternoon he led a sortie – one of several – to capture a gun, but was finally killed, the last of his party to fall. The remaining Guides, whose devoted loyalty had been won by his heroic leadership, fought on, despite offers of safe conduct, until all were killed.

TOP **British officers, Queen's Own Corps of Guides, 1878. Walter Hamilton is at extreme right, standing. Next to him, seated, is Surgeon Kelly, who also fell at the Kabul Residency; seated far left is Wigram Battye, mortally wounded at Futtehabad in 1879, and standing second from right is his brother Fred, killed in 1895 during the relief of Chitral.** (Mrs D.Battye)

ABOVE **Wigram Battye falls at the head of the Guides Cavalry at the battle of Futtehabad, 2 April 1879, after which Walter Hamilton assumed command, and won the Victoria Cross which he never lived to wear.** (P.J.Haythornthwaite)

Hamilton's VC for Futtehabad was formally gazetted a month later – a poignant and undeserved bureaucratic delay over the highest gallantry award to one called 'a noble specimen of a British officer'.

Haldane Rattray

Another Indian Army subaltern who held an independent command defending a remote place was Lieutenant Haldane Burney Rattray of the 45th Sikhs, a regiment that bore his name as a subsidiary title, having been raised by his father just before the Mutiny.

Born in 1870, he was first commissioned in 1890 into the Derbyshire Regiment before transferring to the Indian Army. When the Great Pathan Revolt broke out in 1897 the 45th Sikhs formed part of the important Malakand garrison, with two detached companies ten miles away at Fort Chakdara, guarding a bridge over the River Swat. This was Lieutenant Rattray's command.

The fort was built on a rocky, steep-sided hillock, difficult to assault but overlooked all round by the nearby hills, most within rifle range. Besides his 180 Sikhs, Rattray had 20 Bengal Lancers, later increased by another 40, two Maxims and a 9-pounder gun. Reports had been received of a horde of tribesmen advancing towards Malakand and Chakdara.

On the night of 26 July both garrisons were attacked in great strength. Over the next six days and nights Rattray and his men withstood massed attacks and constant rifle fire from the hills in the

intervals between them. The garrison was outnumbered by eight to one at the start; the enemy numbers daily increased, until by 30 July it was nearer 50 to one. That night attacks at Malakand ceased, but those tribesmen swelled the numbers at Chakdara. There the enemy rifle fire greatly intensified, covering renewed mass attacks. At dawn on 2 August the largest onslaught yet seen – up to 14,000 strong – came on. Rattray and his men, by now all very tired, held them off for two hours but the situation was now critical. Suddenly Indian cavalry were seen crossing the bridge and the tribesmen began to run. Rattray led out a sortie, and received a neck wound from almost the last shot fired. Nevertheless he had held Chakdara for a week against overwhelming odds. He was awarded the DSO – an award, for a subaltern, only just short of a VC.

Rattray remained with his regiment, rising to lieutenant-colonel commanding like his father before him. During the Great War the regiment joined the Mesopotamian Expeditionary Force. On 1 February 1917 the 45th attacked Turkish positions on the River Hai. They cleared

TOP **Chakdara Fort on the River Swat, defended by Lt H.B.Rattray with two companies of the 45th Sikhs against overwhelming odds from 26 July to 2 August 1897 during the Great Pathan Revolt. Drawing by Maj Hobday, RA. (Author's collection)**

ABOVE **Rattray (left, bareheaded) with officers and men of the 45th Sikhs after the relief of Chakdara. The other bareheaded officer nearest Rattray is his subaltern, 2nd Lt L.L.Wheatley. (Rulzion Rattray)**

the first two trenches, but were then counter-attacked. They counter-charged but suffered heavy casualties. Among their dead was Haldane Rattray, of 45th Rattray's Sikhs, a regiment specially commended by the general commanding for its 'magnificent fighting qualities'.

Frederick Roberts

After these examples at the lower end of the Army in India's command structure, next comes probably the most celebrated of Victorian commanders whose long career, embracing both India and Africa, was crowned with an earldom and in which he rose from an HEIC subaltern with the VC to the very highest appointments. **Plate I** depicts Frederick Sleigh Roberts, a man small in size but great in reputation, revered by all ranks, British and Indian – Kipling's 'Bobs Bahadur'.

His family were Anglo-Irish gentry long settled in Co. Waterford, but he was born in 1832 in India where his father became a general in the HEIC's Bengal Army. After schooling at Eton he passed second into Sandhurst, but transferred to the HEIC equivalent, Addiscombe, whence he was commissioned in 1851 into the Bengal Artillery, earning a coveted place three years later in its elite Horse Artillery.

During the Mutiny he experienced much service and his first wound, initially with the Delhi Field Force as a battery officer and staff officer to John Nicholson (see above), whom he greatly admired, and later in the various Lucknow operations, chiefly as a staff officer to Hope Grant (see above). While serving with Grant's cavalry division he won his VC for saving a sowar's life and capturing a standard on 2 January 1858.

His Mutiny service gained him sick-leave (and marriage) in Ireland, his captaincy and brevet-majority. The next 15 years saw his rise to colonel but on the staff, not as a commander. He became particularly proficient in the fields of supply and transport over difficult terrain: on the NW Frontier in 1863 during the sizeable Umbeyla expedition, in Assam against the Lushai in 1871 and, in between, with Sir Robert Napier's Abyssinian campaign of 1868 (see below). His expertise earned him the CB and temporary rank of major-general at General Headquarters India in 1875. Here he became involved in the discussions about the Russian threat and the rival theories as to how it should best be countered, Roberts favouring the 'forward policy' of controlling the Frontier passes and their surrounding tribesmen. This led, in 1878, to his first important command, now aged 56, of the Punjab Frontier Force. Then, when a Russian mission's arrival at Kabul brought on the Second Afghan War, he was given the Kurram Field Force, one of three for the invasion of Afghanistan.

It was his skilful turning of the strong Afghan position on the Peiwar Kotal on 1/2 December 1878 that first made his name as a field commander, earning him the admiration and loyalty of his force and the KCB. His growing reputation was further enhanced by his victory at Charasiah on 6 October 1879, en route for Kabul to avenge the attack on Cavagnari's mission (see Hamilton above), and his subsequent decisive defeat of the Afghan counter-offensive around Kabul, which seemed to end the war.

However, in July 1880 a new threat emerged to the south-west from a fresh Afghan force which, after defeating Burrows' brigade at Maiwand,

Frederick Roberts in 1852, when aged 20 and a subaltern in HEIC Bengal Artillery. Print after a drawing by E.Grimston. (F.Roberts, *Letters written during the Indian Mutiny*)

prepared to besiege the garrison of Kandahar. Then came Roberts' greatest achievement of the war: his famous march with 10,000 men across 313 miles in 22 days from Kabul to Kandahar, culminating in his rout of the enemy on 1 September. Before this war Roberts was hardly known outside the Army in India; after it he was a GCB, a baronet, a lieutenant-general and a national hero.

He became C-in-C in Madras, then of India, from 1885 to 1893. He became much preoccupied with the organisation and infrastructure for India's defence from the north-west, as well as the troops' wellbeing and training for war. On major policy matters he sometimes disagreed with the Army reformers at home led by his chief rival in military fame – Garnet Wolseley (see below). He finally left India in 1893 after 41 years' service there, receiving the barony of Kandahar.

In 1895 he was created field-marshal and C-in-C Ireland. He had reached the top and retirement may have beckoned, but it was not to be. The early disasters of the Boer War in 1899 (see below) demanded a new overall commander. With Wolseley now something of a spent force, there was only one alternative. In December 1899, though aged 67, in indifferent health, and mourning the death in action of his only son – just awarded the VC like his father – Roberts sailed for South Africa.

This, his last and greatest command, more properly belongs in the the later section on Africa; but since his career was predominantly Indian – indeed, in 48 years' service he had never even soldiered in Africa – it is more fitting to complete his career here.

With Kitchener (see below) as his Chief of Staff, Roberts disembarked in January 1900. He quickly perceived the urgent need for more mounted troops; for a better transport system; and, operationally, for an end to reinforcing failure in Natal, and a strike at the Orange Free State (nearest to Cape Colony) before invading the Transvaal and capturing its capital, Pretoria. Despite other pressures he adhered resolutely to this plan. Starting in February, he entered Pretoria in June, having inflicted several defeats upon the Boers. Further operations followed so that, by late October, all the hitherto besieged garrisons had

Roberts' march from Kabul to relieve Kandahar, August 1880, during the Second Afghan War; crossing the Zamburak Kotal. Roberts can be seen to the right, mounted on a grey held by one of his Gurkha orderlies. Besides Indian Army troops, his force included HM 9th Lancers, 60th Rifles, 72nd and 92nd Highlanders. Painting by Chevalier L.W.Desanges. (Royal Artillery Institution)

been relieved, no town of any importance remained in Boer hands, and both Boer republics were annexed. In nine months he had completely reversed the 1899 setbacks and had seemingly won the war. (As will be seen later, this was not so.) He returned home and was rewarded by Queen Victoria in one of her last acts with an earldom and the Order of the Garter.

He became King Edward VII's first C-in-C of the Army until 1904, the last to hold that post, after which the upper control of the Army was remodelled. In his retirement he devoted much time to advocating compulsory military service in preparation for a European war. When war came with Germany in 1914 Roberts joined the Government's War Council. In November the first Indian Army contingent reached France. Roberts crossed the Channel to visit the soldiers and regiments he had known so well. Three days later he caught a chill and died, much mourned, aged 82. He was buried in St Paul's Cathedral.

Francis Brownlow

With Roberts in Plate I are representatives of the two regiments that led the flank attack at Peiwar Kotal in 1878: Lieutenant-Colonel Francis Brownlow, commanding HM 72nd Highlanders, and a rifleman of the 5th Gurkha Regiment.

Brownlow was born in 1836, of parents both connected to the Irish nobility, and was educated at Harrow. He was commissioned ensign by purchase in September 1854 into the 72nd, which reached the Crimea in May 1855. He served in the Kerch expedition and the siege of Sebastopol as a lieutenant, remaining in that rank when the 72nd arrived in India in late 1857 to join the Central India Field Force. At the capture of Kotah in March 1858 Brownlow was in the leading assault column. He obtained his captaincy by purchase in 1862.

He became lieutenant-colonel of the 72nd in 1877. His leading of the regiment at Peiwar Kotal earned him the CB. He and his 72nd continued under Roberts' command throughout the Afghan War, earning his general's commendation as 'a dashing commander' and particularly for his 'brilliant' leadership at the Asmai Heights in the Kabul fighting of

LtCol Francis Brownlow (seated right of window, with stick) and his officers of HM 72nd Highlanders at Kabul in 1880 before the relief of Kandahar. (Queen's Own Highlanders/Seaforth & Camerons)

GENERAL OFFICERS' FULL DRESS
1: Major-General, CB, c.1840
2: General, GCB, c.1870
3: Lieutenant-General, KCB, c.1900

A

INDIA, 1843
1: Major-General Sir Charles Napier, KCB
2: Officer, HEIC Bombay Horse Artillery
3: Sowar, HEIC Sind Irregular Horse

B

INDIA, 1846
1: General Sir Hugh Gough, GCB
2: Major-General Sir Harry Smith, KCB
3: Sergeant Bernard McCabe, HM 31st Regiment

C

THE CRIMEA, 1854
1: Lieutant-Colonel Lacy Yea, HM 7th Royal Fusiliers
2: Brigadier-General Hon. James Scarlett
3: Lieutenant-General Hon. Sir George Cathcart, KCB

THE CRIMEA, 1854
1: Major-General John Pennefather, CB
2: General Lord Raglan, GCB
3: Captain Frederick Haines, HM 21st Royal North British Fusiliers

THE INDIAN MUTINY, 1857-58
1: Brigadier-General John Nicholson
2: Major-General Sir Henry Havelock, KCB
3: Major-General Sir Hope Grant, KCB

F

THE INDIAN MUTINY, 1857-58
1: Lieutenant-General Sir Colin Campbell, GCB
2: Brevet Lieutenant-Colonel John Ewart, HM 93rd Highlanders
3: Sergeant Joe Lee, HM 53rd Regiment

G

JUNIOR COMMANDERS, 1860-97
1: Lieutenant Robert Rogers, HM 44th Regiment; China, 1860
2: Lieutenant Walter Hamilton,
  Queen's Own Corps of Guides (PFF); Kabul, 1879
3: Lieutenant Haldane Rattray, 45th (Rattray's Sikhs),
  Bengal Infantry; NW Frontier, 1897

SECOND AFGHAN WAR, 1878
1: Major-General Frederick Roberts, VC, CB
2: Lieutenant-Colonel Francis Brownlow, HM 72nd Highlanders
3: Sepoy, 5th Gurkha Regiment (PFF)

AFRICA, 1868-84
1: Lieutenant-General Sir Robert Napier, KCB; Abyssinia, 1868
2: Major-General Sir Garnet Wolseley, KCMG, CB; Ashanti expedition, 1873
3: Brigadier-General Sir Herbert Stewart, KCB; Sudan, 1884

J

ZULULAND, 1879
1: Colonel Evelyn Wood, VC
2: Lieutenant-Colonel Redvers Buller
3: Bugler Walkinshaw, 90th Light Infantry

SUDAN, 1898
1: Major-General Sir Herbert Kitchener, KCB, KCMG
2: Colonel Hector MacDonald, DSO
3: Askari, Xth Sudanese Battalion, Egyptian Army

December 1879. Sadly he was killed in the last battle of the war, at Kandahar, while leading his Highlanders to clear some strongly-held enclosures. His death, Roberts recorded, was 'a great loss', much felt by all the 72nd, and especially by his widow whom he had married only two years before and who was left with an infant son.

The 5th Gurkhas, part of the PFF, served alongside the 72nd in all Roberts' Afghan battles. The soldier in Plate I represents one of two Gurkha orderlies from the 5th who, with two Pathans and two Sikhs, always attended Roberts in Afghanistan, providing him with information and close protection. One of these Gurkhas later became Subadar of the 5th.

AFRICA

Campaigns, 1837-98, in Outline

The Army's operations in Africa during the Victorian epoch began in Cape Colony with the Seventh and Eighth Kaffir or Frontier Wars, mentioned earlier in the careers of Sir Harry Smith and Sir George Cathcart.

The next involvement occurred much further north in Abyssinia, where an expedition from India landed in 1868 to secure the release of European hostages held by the Emperor Theodore. West Africa featured next, with the 1873-74 campaign against the northern Ashanti tribes' incursions against the coastal peoples and trading settlements of the Gold Coast.

In Southern Africa the last of the Frontier Wars in 1877-78 was followed a year later by the invasion and conquest of Zululand, to pre-empt a perceived threat to Natal and to further British plans for confederation in the region – an unjustified venture which began with disaster for British arms. Further defeats followed in 1881 when the Boers of the Transvaal, annexed by Britain in 1877 as part of confederation, rebelled and regained their independence.

The battle of El Teb, Eastern Sudan, 29 February 1884; the 10th Royal Hussars charging with Herbert Stewart's Cavalry Brigade. Painting by G.D.Giles. (The Royal Hussars)

The focus of military activity then shifted north to Egypt, nominally part of the Ottoman Empire but with Anglo-French control of its finances. In 1882 a military, nationalist coup led to fears for the security of the strategically vital Suez Canal in which Britain had a controlling interest. The despatch of an expeditionary force from Britain and India restored the status quo of the Khedive's rule, underpinned by a British military and administrative presence and the reform of the Egyptian Army under British leadership.

The burden of military involvement in Egypt increased with the Mahdist Revolt in the Sudan against Egyptian rule. Assistance was at first confined to the despatch of one general – Charles Gordon; but when he became besieged in Khartoum in 1884 a relief expedition was belatedly despatched up the Nile while other forces in the Eastern Sudan, including Indian and Australian troops, fought two small campaigns to secure the Red Sea port of Suakin. The Nile force was too late to save Gordon, and in 1885 the government ordered the evacuation of the Sudan, except for Suakin. Occasional fighting occurred on the Egyptian frontier thereafter, but it was not until 1898 that an Anglo-Egyptian army reconquered the Sudan after a two-year campaign.

The South African War in Outline

The Victorian era closed with its third major conflict, the South African or Anglo-Boer War, fought against the two Boer Republics of the Orange Free State and the Transvaal by the British Army (including its Reserve Army units – Militia and Volunteers), reinforced by contingents from Australia, Canada, New Zealand and South Africa itself, but without the Indian Army [1]. Hostilities fell into three main phases:

October-December 1899 The Boers advance into Natal and Cape Colony and besiege Ladysmith, Mafeking and Kimberley. British failures and defeats while trying to relieve these garrisons.

January-October 1900 Roberts appointed C-in-C. British counter-offensive into, first, Orange Free State, then Transvaal, supported by Buller's advance from Natal, culminating in annexation of both Boer Republics.

November 1900-May 1902 Boers conduct guerrilla campaign. Kitchener's counter-measures eventually procure Boer surrender.

Of British commanders prominent in this war, Roberts has been covered above, and three more follow below but are pictured in the Plates as they appeared in earlier African campaigns.

Lord Roberts, Commander-in-Chief in South Africa, with his Chief of Staff Lord Kitchener, entering Pretoria, capital of the Transvaal, on 4 June 1900. *(Famous Men and Battles of the British Empire)*

1 This war has been more fully covered in other Osprey publications:
    Men-at-Arms 303, *Boer Wars (2) 1898-1902*;
    Martin Marix Evans' *The Boer War: South Africa 1899-1902*.

COMMANDERS

Robert Napier

Although **Plate J** shows Lieutenant-General Sir Robert Napier, KCB, as commander of the 1868 Abyssinian expedition, his career as a whole was more Indian than African, thus linking this section to those preceding it.

A distant cousin of Charles Napier (see above), he was born in Ceylon in 1810, the son of an HEIC major. He was commissioned from Addiscombe in 1826 into the HEIC Bengal Engineers. As a captain he commanded engineers in the battles of the First Sikh War and was wounded when he accompanied HM 31st in their attack at Ferozeshah, receiving a brevet-majority. In the second war he was Chief Engineer at the siege of Multan and was also at the final victory of Gujerat, receiving his next brevet. His subsequent appointment as the Punjab's chief civil engineer was interrupted in 1852 by his first field command of other arms in one of the earliest NW Frontier campaigns, against the Black Mountain tribes. His column, which included the Guides (see Hamilton above), encountered the stiffest opposition but his tactical handling dispersed the enemy. In 1854 he gained his third brevet, to colonel.

During the Mutiny he acted as the senior staff officer in Havelock's force which reinforced Lucknow, and was wounded during Campbell's second relief. Promoted brigadier-general, he commanded a brigade of engineers during Campbell's recapture of Lucknow in March 1858. He then became Sir Hugh Rose's deputy in the Central India Field Force during the operations in Gwalior and the final capture of Tantia Tope in 1859, being advanced to KCB.

Now recognised as an experienced and able higher commander, he was given the 2nd Division in Sir Hope Grant's 1860 China force, being promoted major-general; and in 1865 he took over the Bombay Army. There followed his first major independent command: of the 15,000-strong force – with a vast number of logistic 'followers' and baggage animals – found by the Bombay Army for the Abyssinian expedition of 1868 after all diplomatic efforts to free Theodore's hostages had failed.

This expedition posed very considerable tactical and particularly logistical problems, from the landing of the force from 280 ships on a coast with no harbour, through the establishment of a base and the subsequent 400-mile advance through unknown country against an unpredictable enemy, to the final capture of Magdala. However, Napier's excellent organisation and handling of the operations ensured complete success and with

Robert, 1st Baron Napier of Magdala as a lieutenant-general, GCB, GCSI in c.1870. (P.J.Haythornthwaite)

The last act of Sir Robert Napier's Abyssinian campaign: the storming of Emperor Theodore's fortress at Magdala, 13 April 1868, led by Royal Engineers, Madras Sappers and Miners, and HM 33rd Regiment. (J.Grant, *British Battles on Land and Sea*)

remarkably few casualties, making it one of the best-conducted African campaigns of the period.

Napier was rewarded with a barony, of Magdala, the GCSI and GCB. He became C-in-C India from 1870 to 1876 and Governor of Gibraltar from 1876 to 1883, finishing that appointment with promotion to field-marshal. Like Roberts after him, Napier was another HEIC officer – a 'lesser breed' in the Queen's Army's eyes – who achieved the very highest rank, and after more active service than many in the latter Army. Among other achievements he fathered 15 children, six of his nine sons becoming officers in the British or Indian Armies. He died in 1890.

Garnet Wolseley

Another who accomplished two successful African campaigns in independent command, and who saw much varied warfare as a regimental and a staff officer, Garnet Joseph Wolseley was held in some late Victorian military circles to be 'our only General'. He is pictured in Plate J on the scene of the first of his African successes, the Ashanti War of 1873-74, a campaign which launched his career as a general officer whose prestige at home and in Africa was to rival Roberts' in India.

He was born in 1823 in Dublin, son of a major in HM 25th Regiment and his Protestant Irish wife, a religious woman of strong character. The father died when Wolseley was only seven, leaving the widow and six other children in reduced circumstances. Wolseley was determined to enter the Army but purchasing a commission was out of the question. Eventually pleading letters to the Duke of Wellington, then C-in-C of the Army, secured him an ensigncy in HM 80th. During the Second Burma War of 1851-53 he distinguished himself while leading an attack on a stockade, but was badly wounded and invalided home.

When fit again he transferred to HM 90th Light Infantry, remaining the rein for the rest of his regimental service, and fighting with it at the siege of Sebastopol, being twice wounded and losing an eye, and later in the Mutiny during Campbell's Lucknow operations. He was often mentioned in despatches in both campaigns, earning an early captaincy when aged only 21. Whilst in the Crimean trenches he met a Sapper subaltern with whom he began a lifelong friendship – Charles Gordon. At Lucknow, when raising a flag on a building upon which he had just led the assault, he found himself assisted by a Gunner subaltern – Frederick Roberts – the second of two chance encounters of later significance.

After Lucknow's final capture Wolseley was posted to Sir Hope Grant's divisional staff for the Oudh campaign, work which was rewarded with a brevet lieutenant-colonelcy

Capt Garnet Wolseley, HM 90th LI, rescuing the wounded Pte Andrews while storming the Moti Mahal on 17 November 1857 during the second relief of Lucknow. Painting by W.B.Wollen. (*Illustrated Naval and Military Magazine,* 1885)

when still only 25. He continued with Grant throughout the 1860 China War, adding to his reputation both as a courageous and intelligent leader of soldiers and a most able staff officer. After only eight years' service he was clearly a 'coming man'.

From 1861 he served on the staff in Canada, rising to full colonel and, when off duty, studying his profession deeply, including some writing on the China War and on the American Civil War, of which he saw something at first hand. His most famous publication was *The Soldier's Pocket Book*, a manual of organisation and tactics. His Canadian tour ended with his first independent command, of the 1870 Red River Expedition against rebellious French Canadians; this was a logistic rather than a tactical challenge, but its success earned him the KCMG and CB.

In 1871 he began the first of several increasingly influential Whitehall appointments which coincided with the Cardwell Reforms aimed at modernising the Army, of which Wolseley became a leading supporter. This work was interrupted by his triumph with the Ashanti Expedition, a campaign as much against climate and terrain as King Kofi's warriors, which he speedily terminated. It earned him a GCMG and KCB, and a growing national reputation as the epitome of the 'Modern Major-General', whose efficiency made everything 'all Sir Garnet'. This campaign also witnessed the start of the 'Wolseley Ring'; these were a group of his specially selected subordinates whose future careers became linked with his – a phenomenon that would provoke disfavour in some reactionary circles.

His continuing Whitehall career was further interrupted by largely administrative posts in Natal (1875) and Cyprus (1878), by which time he was a lieutenant-general at the age of only 45. He returned to South Africa in 1879 to take over the Zulu War after its early setbacks, but the Zulus were defeated before he arrived, leaving him with a mainly administrative task.

After this he returned to the more congenial and third most senior Whitehall post of Quartermaster-General, moving up to Adjutant-General in 1882, an appointment he held until 1890 (though twice interrupted by his last two field commands). His reforming zeal for measures such as shorter Regular service coupled with a period on the Reserve, the localisation of the infantry, affiliation of Regular and Auxiliary units, more realistic training, and greater professionalism were all to fit the Army for modern warfare. However, combined with his abrasive manner, they incurred the hostility of the conservative elements

LtGen Sir Garnet Wolseley and his staff at the close of the battle of Tel-el-Kebir, 13 September 1882, being cheered by Gordon and Cameron Highlanders. After the painting by Lady Butler (now destroyed). (FM E.Wood, VC, *British Battles on Land and Sea*)

FM Viscount Wolseley, KP, GCB, OM, GCMG, in full dress in 1895 when he became the last but one Commander-in-Chief of the British Army before that appointment was discontinued. (P.J.Haythornthwaite)

led by the C-in-C, the Duke of Cambridge, and to some extent of the 'Indians' led by Roberts. Furthermore, his 'Ring' naturally alienated those who were not part of it.

Nevertheless, none could gainsay his success as a field commander when he temporarily left Whitehall to command the Egyptian expedition in 1882 against Arabi Pasha's revolt. This masterly campaign culminated in the victory of Tel-el-Kebir, for which he received a barony, of Cairo, and promotion to full general.

Two years later he again took the field, after much procrastination by Gladstone's government, with his Nile expedition of desert and river columns to attempt the relief of his old friend Gordon in Khartoum. Wolseley blamed its failure on Gladstone, not, in his book, the 'Grand Old Man' but the 'Murderer of Gordon'. The expedition was also beset by jealousies and arguments between members of his 'Ring', all now quite senior and less responsive to Wolseley's orders.

This setback (which was nevertheless rewarded with a viscountcy) and continuing difficulties in Whitehall began to take their toll of Wolseley's forceful and innovative powers. He left the War Office in 1890 to become C-in-C Ireland; was promoted field-marshal in 1894; and the following year succeeded Cambridge as Commander-in-Chief, although by then the post had become subject to closer political control. The efficient organisation, mobilisation and despatch of the army corps for South Africa in 1899 vindicated his years of modernising work, but its early failures in the field showed that much – including what he had preached but had not been acted upon – remained to be done. This would be fully rectified between 1902 and 1914. Wolseley finally retired in 1900, handing over to his rival Roberts, and died in 1913.

Herbert Stewart

One of Wolseley's protégés was Sir Herbert Stewart. He spent most of his career on the staff, often serving Wolseley who described him as 'one of the best staff officers' he had known, and only received his first commands in the last year of his life.

Born in 1843, the son of a Hampshire clergyman, he was educated at Winchester and began his career in 1863 as an infantryman in HM 37th Regiment, rising to captain by 1868. After spending five years in staff posts in India he returned home in 1873, transferred to the cavalry in the 3rd Dragoon Guards, and entered the Staff College.

An uninspiring staff job in the Zulu War left him somewhat disillusioned with his career until the arrival of Wolseley who, spotting his worth, made him his military secretary, that work securing him a brevet lieutenant-colonelcy. Misfortune followed when, as chief staff officer to Sir

George Colley in the Transvaal War, he was captured at Majuba Hill, though released soon afterwards.

This did not damage his career, for in 1882 he was appointed chief staff officer in the Cavalry Division of Wolseley's force for Egypt. He was present at Kassassin and, after the victory at Tel-el-Kebir, rode on ahead of his division with only 50 cavalrymen to Cairo, where he skilfully secured the surrender of its large garrison and of Arabi Pasha himself. For this and all his work in the campaign he was made CB and a brevet colonel.

Stewart's growing reputation won him command of the cavalry – 10th and 19th Hussars and some mounted infantry – in Gen Graham's expedition to the Eastern Sudan in 1884. At his first battle, El Teb, thinking the enemy were retreating, he led a fine charge in pursuit; but his rear squadrons were attacked by concealed tribesmen, and it was only by dismounted fire that success was finally achieved, though at some cost. At Tamai, however, he saved a broken infantry brigade's square from heavy loss by his swift advance and dismounted action against the enemy's flank. After this short campaign Stewart was made KCB.

Later that year Wolseley summoned him for the Gordon Relief Expedition and gave him command of the Desert Column, of four camel-mounted regiments, to cut across the desert from Korti to Metemmeh prior to making the final 96-mile dash to Khartoum while the River Column proceeded up the Nile. It is in this command that he is pictured in Plate J. On 17 January 1885 his camel corps, formed in square, were heavily attacked near Abu Klea. The Mahdists broke into the square at one point, but the force survived to continue the advance. Two days later they came under rifle fire and Stewart received a mortal wound. He had to hand over to the next senior, an efficient intelligence officer but lacking the drive and command experience vital at this juncture. Stewart survived long enough to learn that Khartoum had fallen but that he had been promoted major-general. Wolseley wrote of him: 'No braver soldier or more brilliant leader ever wore the Queen's uniform'.

In **Plate K** are two prominent members of Wolseley's 'Ring' as they appeared in the Zulu War before Wolseley arrived: Colonel Henry Evelyn Wood, VC, as commander of No.4 or Left Column; and Lieutenant-Colonel Redvers Henry Buller, 60th Rifles, commanding the Frontier Light Horse and other Colonial mounted units in Wood's column, who won the VC in that capacity.

Evelyn Wood

Wood was born in 1838, the son of an Essex vicar, and was educated at Marlborough before entering the Royal Navy. Serving ashore in the

TOP **Sir Herbert Stewart as a lieutenant-colonel in the undress uniform of the 3rd Dragoon Guards, c.1880. From a photograph. (*The Graphic,* 1885)**

ABOVE **The Desert Column under rifle fire near Metemmeh on 19 January 1885, when BrigGen Stewart sustained his mortal wound. Eyewitness drawing by Lt Count E.Gleichen, Guards Camel Regiment. (E.Gleichen, *With the Camel Corps up the Nile*)**

Crimea as a 16-year-old midshipman, he was badly wounded during the assault on Sebastopol, being recommended, unsuccessfully, for the VC. He was invalided home, but his gallantry won him a change of service, with a cornetcy in HM 13th Light Dragoons, exchanging as a lieutenant in 1857 into HM 17th Lancers to see service in the Mutiny.

During the Central India campaign two acts of gallantry – charging some mutineers single-handed, and later saving a loyal Indian's life – did win him the VC and a reputation for 'indomitable energy and great daring'. The climate, however, caused him much ill-health, from which he was to suffer all his life (aggravated by some degree of hypochondria).

Returning to England he graduated from the Staff College. Having served on the staff he left the cavalry for the infantry, purchasing a majority in HM 90th Light Infantry in 1871; this was Wolseley's old regiment, where his abilities were noted by that officer. When Wolseley was organising his Ashanti expedition he selected Wood to raise a West African regiment. This Wood led with distinction throughout the campaign, being again wounded but mentioned in despatches five times. Afterwards he received a CB, a brevet colonelcy and an assured place in the 'Ring'.

Wood's reputation was further enhanced by his command of the 90th in the Ninth Frontier War, which resulted in his appointment in the Zulu War to lead No.4 Column, containing his own 90th (now under Rogers, see above), the 13th Light Infantry and Buller's Colonial Horse. After the early disaster to the Centre Column at Isandhlwana, Wood evened the score with his battles at Hlobane and Kambula, inflicting serious losses on the Zulus. In the second invasion of Zululand Wood's column led the advance to Ulundi and held the right face of the square in the final victory. Probably the most effective commander of the war, he was made KCB and earned his superior Chelmsford's tribute for having 'never spared himself although suffering severely in bodily health'.

Wood returned to South Africa in 1881 as Colley's deputy in the Transvaal War. After assuming overall command following Colley's death at Majuba, he found he was constrained from further military action by the Gladstone government's instructions to negotiate peace with the Boers and oversee the settlement of the Transvaal. This proved an unwelcome task since he had made ready to re-open hostilities, but for

The battle of Kambula, 29 March 1879, where Evelyn Wood's No.4 or Left Column defeated the Zulus attacking his laager. Watercolour by Orlando Norie. (County Museum, Taunton)

which he was made GCMG and promoted major-general.

The following year Wolseley gave him the 4th Division for the Egyptian War and the independent role of diverting the enemy forces around Alexandria while the main army made the outflanking thrust via the Suez Canal that ended with Tel-el-Kebir. After the war he was given the task of reorganising the Egyptian Army. The results he achieved in two years' work laid the foundation of its later successes, as will be seen. While he was still so employed Wolseley again required his services to organise the lines of communication for the Gordon Relief Expedition and, after Khartoum's fall, to take over as his chief of staff in place of Buller (see below).

His health had again deteriorated so badly that he needed a year to recover. After the Sudan he never served overseas again, but he held important commands at the major military centres at home, Colchester and Aldershot, where he did much to improve training, shooting, the mounted infantry arm (whose worth he had long advocated), and the Auxiliary forces, and introduced measures to better the lot of the ordinary soldier, whom he always held in high regard.

This latter work he carried on when, as a lieutenant-general and GCB from 1893, he became Quartermaster-General at the War Office, where he also reorganised the system of transporting troops; and later as Adjutant-General, with responsibility for mobilisation before the Boer War. In all these appointments he gave whole-hearted support for Wolseley's modernisation plans for the Army.

His last command, as a full general, was of the 2nd Army Corps based on the new training area of Salisbury Plain. He became a field-marshal in 1903 and, notwithstanding his long history of illness, he survived until the age of 81, dying in 1919.

Wolseley, while acknowledging all Wood's qualities of courage, industry, stoicism and progressive professionalism, considered him vain and self-seeking. Nevertheless Wood thought deeply about his profession, as revealed in his several published books, particularly his two-volume autobiography, and military articles; and, unlike some generals, he always enjoyed an excellent rapport with his men.

Illustrating this quality in Plate K is Wood's orderly, Bugler Walkinshaw who, with eight mounted infantrymen of the 90th, formed his permanent escort during the Zulu War. Wood, no mean judge of courage, thought Walkinshaw 'one of the bravest men in the Army', and that he would have won the VC at Hlobane – as did two others – had not Wood called him back. He was, however, awarded the DCM. At the end of the war Wood entertained him and the others of the escort at a dinner in Pietermaritzburg, a thoughtful and unusual reward. Walkinshaw remained in Wood's service after the Zulu War, earning his officer's

Gen Sir Evelyn Wood, VC, GCB, GCMG, aged 63 in 1901 when Adjutant-General to the Forces. He is wearing general officer's full dress but with undress forage cap. (P.J.Haythornthwaite)

tribute and gratitude in his autobiography for the orderly's devotion, especially when Wood was so ill in the Sudan.

Redvers Buller

Buller received a major independent command towards the end of his 48 years' commissioned service when aged 60, a command larger than any other mentioned in this book. Yet previously he had only held two field commands: once as a lieutenant-colonel of Colonial levies, the other as a brigadier in a two-month campaign. The rest of his service, after leaving regimental duty as a captain, had been on the staff – sometimes in action rather than behind a desk, but not as a commander. Nevertheless the magnitude of his last command qualifies him for inclusion here, as it did Raglan.

Born in 1839 into gentry long established in Devon, he was educated at Eton and commissioned in 1858 into HM 60th Rifles, with whom he always remained associated. He served with its different battalions in India, in the 1860 China War, and twice in Canada. With its 1st Battalion he was in the Red River Expedition of 1870 where, as a captain, he first attracted Wolseley's notice as 'a thorough soldier'. He entered the Staff College in late 1871 but never completed the course, as he was summoned by Wolseley to join the Ashanti expedition as chief intelligence officer, for which he was subsequently awarded the CB, a brevet majority and continuing membership of the 'Ring'.

After his first spell in the War Office he went out to the Ninth Frontier War and was given command of the Frontier Light Horse, a mixed bag of Colonial volunteers which he welded into an effective unit, thereby earning a brevet lieutenant-colonelcy. With this unit and other mounted auxiliaries he joined Wood's column for the Zulu War. At Hlobane Mountain he found himself greatly outnumbered and in danger of being cut off. During his retreat, at great personal risk, he saved the lives of two officers and a trooper who had been unhorsed. For this he was awarded the VC on Wood's recommendation. He remained with Wood's column for the rest of the war, afterwards being made CMG and a colonel.

He worked closely with Wood again in South Africa as chief of staff after the Majuba fiasco. The following year he returned to Wolseley's side as his chief of intelligence for the Egyptian War, during which his personal reconnaissance of the Tel-el-Kebir positions contributed to Wolseley's convincing victory. Thereafter he became KCMG.

A cigarette card commemorating the Victoria Cross won by LtCol Redvers Buller on 28 March 1879 when pursued by Zulus during the retreat from Hlobane, in which he saved three men's lives. (Author's collection)

Col. Sir. F
Capt. D
inhlobani Mountain

Jessica,
Please remind me to
talk to you about this
order. No Big Deal its just
easier than writing out a
big long explanation.

Ben

255 Grossman Drive • Braintree, MA 02184
(617) 356-5111

Printed on Recycled Paper

Another brief tour in the War Office was followed by his second command, of a brigade in Gen Graham's 1884 campaign in the Eastern Sudan (see Stewart above), fighting at El Teb and Tamai. At Tamai his brigade, which included the 3rd Battalion of his old 60th, helped save the other brigade's broken square by advancing on its right and dispersing the enemy with controlled volleys while Stewart's cavalry acted on its left. Buller's coolness under fire and his firm control of his three battalions helped turn a near-disaster into the enemy's rout, for which he was promoted major-general.

He was summoned again by Wolseley to be his chief of staff for the Nile expedition, an appointment Wolseley later regretted, finding him argumentative, opinionated, hostile to Stewart, and not always reliable. Belatedly Wolseley decided Buller was more suited to command than staff work and, after Khartoum's fall, sent him to take over the Desert Column from Stewart's ineffective successor, though by then there was little Buller could do but withdraw.

After this ill-fated campaign, for which he was made KCB, and a year in Ireland aiding the civil power, Buller spent eleven years in the War Office, rising to Quartermaster-General, then Adjutant-General, until 1897, by which date he had become a full general and GCB.

In 1898 he took over the Aldershot Command. The following year he was appointed to command the Army Corps sent out to fight the Boers. Forced by early Boer successes on three fronts into responding to their operations rather than initiating offensives against them, he split up his corps between Natal, Cape Colony and the Kimberley front, becoming himself centred on the relief of Ladysmith. The defeats of 'Black Week' followed, and he recommended the Ladysmith garrison's surrender – which it ignored.

Roberts was sent out to take over as C-in-C and Buller was relegated to a subordinate command purely in Natal. This post he retained with mixed fortunes, including his eventual relief of Ladysmith, until the guerrilla phase of the war began in October 1900, when he went home. He had initially accepted the chief command reluctantly and his misgivings had generally proved justified, yet for all his setbacks he never lost the trust and affection of his troops.

In early 1901, when back at Aldershot, he made a public response to criticisms of his South African command, for which he was removed from his post and never re-employed. Nor was he promoted field-marshal like his contemporaries Wolseley, Wood and of course Roberts, not to mention the defender of Ladysmith, Sir George White VC. Buller died in 1908, mourned by the public and ordinary soldiers despite his critics.

Plate L features two more commanders of the South African War but depicts them a year earlier, during the reconquest of the Sudan by an Anglo-Egyptian army in 1898: the commander of the 1st Egyptian Army Brigade, Colonel Hector MacDonald, DSO, with a soldier from one of his Sudanese battalions; and that army's overall commander, Lieutenant-General Sir Herbert Kitchener, KCB, KCMG.

Gen Sir Redvers Buller, VC, GCB, KCMG, in c.1900, uniformed as Colonel Commandant, King's Royal Rifle Corps (60th Rifles). (P.J.Haythornthwaite)

Hector MacDonald

MacDonald was one of those mentioned in the Introduction who rose from the ranks to achieve distinction as an officer and a commander.

A crofter's son from Ross-shire, he was born in 1853 and enlisted in HM 92nd (Gordon) Highlanders in 1870. Showing a natural aptitude for soldiering, he attained the rank of colour-sergeant, the senior NCO of his company, after only nine years' service, in time for the Second Afghan War. The 92nd was in Roberts' force that advanced to and fought around Kabul in October 1879, actions in which MacDonald's leadership and courage were so outstanding that he was recommended for a commission in the field. This was not only granted but – unusually in such cases – as a subaltern in his own 92nd, where he was warmly welcomed by his brother-officers, continuing with the regiment during Roberts' march to relieve Kandahar.

After this campaign the 92nd was sent to the Transvaal War, arriving in time for Majuba. There MacDonald held out on a knoll with 20 men until all were killed or wounded, MacDonald himself being captured after a last struggle with his fists. He was later released, complete with his presentation broadsword which the Boers returned to him.

He served with his regiment in Wolseley's River Column on the Nile in 1884, thereafter transferring to the new Egyptian Army, rising to *bimbashi* (major) by 1888 and command of a Sudanese battalion. He led it in actions on the Egyptian frontier, receiving a DSO and a majority in the Royal Fusiliers, though remaining with the Egyptian Army.

In 1896 Kitchener, by then *sirdar* (C-in-C) of that army, appointed MacDonald to a Sudanese brigade of three battalions which he led most ably at Firket, Abu Hamed and Atbara. At the final battle, Omdurman, MacDonald and his brigade saved the rear of Kitchener's army from a sudden and unexpected onslaught by 20,000 Mahdists. His masterly handling of a perilous situation won him a colonelcy in the British Army, a CB, appointment as ADC to the Queen, and national acclaim when he returned home.

From a major-general's appointment in the Punjab he went to South Africa in early 1900 to take over the Highland Brigade after its Magersfontein disaster. He restored its morale and led it successfully at Paardeberg and on to Pretoria. By then, after spending 16 years' continuous service in hot climates, he was in poor health and was invalided home, where he was received by the new King and made KCB.

Now Sir Hector, he undertook a tour of Australia and New Zealand to render official

gratitude for their parts in the Boer War, and then returned to India. There some animosity towards this much-elevated ex-ranker seems to have surfaced, and he was posted to a military backwater as GOC Ceylon. In Ceylon's small British community gossip flourished; it culminated in allegations of MacDonald's homosexuality. He returned to England, saw Roberts and the King, then decided he would go back and face a court-martial. However, while passing through Paris he saw an American newspaper reporting his case. He went to his hotel room and shot himself. He was buried in Edinburgh in 1903, 30,000 of his countrymen filing past his grave in tribute – a tragic end for one who had risen, entirely by his abilities, from obscurity to fame.

Herbert Kitchener

Herbert Horatio Kitchener, born in 1850 the son of a colonel who had settled in Ireland, was commissioned into the Royal Engineers in 1871. After serving at home he began a somewhat unusual career which kept him for many years in the Near and Middle East, beginning with survey work in Palestine and Cyprus and continuing, mostly with the Egyptian Army, in Egypt, East Africa and the Sudan, which took him to the end of the century.

Whilst on leave from Cyprus during Wolseley's 1882 Egyptian campaign he undertook some unofficial and covert reconnaissances in disguise. Two years later he did similar work up the Nile as Wolseley's intelligence officer, trying to establish communication with Gordon in Khartoum and guiding Stewart's Desert Column. He had by then transferred to the new Egyptian Army.

Herbert Kitchener when a major, Royal Engineers, c.1885, aged about 35. (P.J.Haythornthwaite)

He left that army in 1885 as a brevet lieutenant-colonel but later returned, first as governor of the Eastern Sudan, running the operations against the local Mahdist leader Osman Digna, and then as Adjutant-General. In 1889, when the main Mahdist army threatened to invade Egypt, Kitchener was given command of the Egyptian cavalry in a force deployed to meet it. Following the Mahdist defeat at Toski he was made CB. He next reorganised the Egyptian Police; then, in 1892, he became *sirdar* (C-in-C) of their Army, increasing its strength and fighting potential for the reconquest of the Sudan by the formation of several Sudanese battalions.

The first phase of that campaign, begun in 1896, was fought entirely by the Egyptian Army and was completed by Kitchener's victory at Firket and the occupation of Dongola Province, for which, now a major-general, he was made KCB. Using the winter to make further preparations, he despatched a force under Major-General Hunter to seize Abu Hamed and Berber, prior to constructing a desert railway southwards from Wadi Halfa for the speedy conveyance of reinforcements and supplies.

By January 1898 Kitchener's Egyptian troops had been strengthened by Major-General Gatacre's British brigade, and in April he defeated Emir Mahmud's 20,000 men on the Atbara. Joined by another British brigade in August, Kitchener advanced up the Nile and destroyed the Mahdist army at Omdurman on 1 September, though not before the day had been saved by Macdonald (see above). A final ceremony in Khartoum marked the end of the Mahdist revolt and the avenging of Gordon, thus fulfilling Kitchener's 13-year-old resolve. His great achievement ended with his peaceful halting of French ambitions on the

57

Kitchener, as C-in-C South Africa (seated second from right), and the Boer general Louis Botha (on Kitchener's right), with their staffs at the Middleburg conference of 28 February 1901 which attempted, but failed, to end the South African War. (H.W.Wilson, *After Pretoria – The Guerilla War*)

Upper Nile at Fashoda. After returning home to receive a barony, of Khartoum, and great public acclaim, he went back to complete the pacification and administration of the Sudan in 1899.

He went from the Sudan to South Africa as Chief of Staff to Roberts after Buller's reverses, though he sometimes acted more as deputy commander in Roberts' absence. For instance, he launched the original attacks on Cronje's laager at Paardeberg; these failed due to his faulty dispositions, before Roberts arrived and converted failure into success. Of course Kitchener's operational experience had hitherto been confined to a largely spear-and-sword enemy using massed formations, inferior in armaments and tactics to the highly mobile Boers. However, he had most efficiently reorganised the force's transport and the mounted arm before Roberts' offensive began. He always displayed huge energy and, when not working at Roberts' headquarters, organised successful operations to safeguard the lines of communication during the advance to Pretoria.

After Roberts' departure at the apparent end of conventional fighting, Kitchener became C-in-C only to find the war still continuing in a guerrilla campaign. He set about this vigorously, establishing lines of block-houses with mobile columns operating in between, while simultaneously depriving the commandos of supplies by burning their farms and herding their families into unhealthy concentration camps – which later attracted much criticism for the high death rate suffered by the internees. The Boers proved a determined and elusive enemy, but Kitchener persevered as determinedly, and eventually forced their surrender in May 1902. He went home to receive a viscountcy and the Order of Merit.

By then, of course, he was no longer one of Queen Victoria's commanders as she had died in 1901, so the rest of his career will be briefly summarised. He was C-in-C India (where he had never previously served) from 1902 to 1909, where he did much to modernise the Army in India both for its defence and for the Great War to come. He was made field-marshal in 1910 and returned to Egypt as chief British administrator. In August 1914 he became Secretary of State for War to huge public satisfaction as the nation prepared itself for the great conflict with Germany. His tenure of that high office inspired both criticism and praise, but his name will always be associated with that New Army of 3,000,000 volunteers which he raised to supplement the old Regular and Territorial Armies. He was lost at sea in June 1916 aboard the torpedoed HMS *Hampshire* while on his way to stiffen the Russian government and army.

Never popular in the Army like Roberts, and often much feared, he was always tireless and single-minded in every task he undertook. Of all the commanders mentioned in this book, only Roberts rivalled him in honours bestowed for service to his country.

CONCLUSION

From the Napoleonic Wars to the South African War, and even into the Great War, these years of warfare have spanned the careers and achievements of some of the notable commanders of Queen Victoria's reign. There were, of course, others, but space has precluded a comprehensive survey.

In rank these men have ranged from lieutenant, including one whose promising career was sadly cut short in that rank, to field-marshal, one of that rank also dying in the field; two began their careers as private soldiers. Some were originally infantrymen, fewer were cavalrymen, several were both, whilst two were sappers and one a gunner. A few started their careers in the Indian Army or its predecessor, the East India Company's Armies, and two saw much service in the British-trained Egyptian Army. The soldiers they commanded were from these armies, and of course the Queen's Army, plus in some cases those from other countries of the British Empire. Five of them had won the Victoria Cross in their younger days, others received lesser gallantry awards.

Their social backgrounds varied from the working class to the aristocracy, though most were public school-educated from the upper middle or professional classes, many of them sons of officers. Nearly half hailed from Ireland, or had Irish connections, while of the remainder Scotland could claim one half, the English countryside the other, though several of the whole were born in India. Most though not all were married, but little or nothing has been said about their wives and families for reasons of space – save one, but she, though a foreigner and first met on a battlefield, was perhaps the most dedicated to 'following the drum'.

These commanders' wars were fought initially with muzzle-loading muskets and cannon, and ended with magazine rifles, machine guns, and quick-firing field guns and howitzers, using fighting formations progressing from line, column and square to skirmishing lines and open order (although the square and close order proved of lasting value against savage enemies encountered en masse). The foes they fought were of great variety: the Imperial Russian Army and European-modelled forces like the Sikh Khalsa, the mutinied Bengal regiments, and regular Afghan and pre-1882 Egyptian troops; the more primitively armed but undaunted massed warriors of Africa, north and south; the formidable and ruthless Pathan tribes of the North-West Frontier; and finally, quite unlike any of the others and perhaps the most redoubtable, the mounted riflemen of the Boer commandos. None were easy to defeat; all required the best endeavours of our commanders and their troops. In no other period of our Army's history has such a variety of campaigning been encountered.

Given that last fact, and their differences in rank, it would be invidious, if not impossible, to attempt any order of merit for them. All received honours and awards and, unless they fell in action, most were promoted to the highest ranks, eight to the highest of all – the now abolished rank of field-marshal.

All were of a now-bygone breed: men who gave their utmost, often their health and sometimes their lives, not for personal gain but out of duty, to Queen, Country and their Army. It is hoped these brief biographies may have whetted the reader's appetite to learn more about them.

BIBLIOGRAPHY

The following list is by no means comprehensive but includes, as recommended for further reading, some general works, some autobiographies or journals, and some biographies whose publication dates should render them obtainable from libraries. Some explanation as to content is added where necessary.

Anglesey, Marquess of, *History of the British Cavalry, Vol.2: 1851-71* (1975). **Campbell, Grant, Scarlett**

ibid, Vol.3: 1872-98 (1982) – **Buller, Roberts, Stewart, Wolseley, Wood**

Barthorp, Michael, *The Frontier Ablaze: The North-West Frontier, 1897-98* (1996) – includes **Rattray**

Battye, Evelyn Desirée, *The Fighting Ten* (1984) – chiefly the Battye brothers but includes **Hamilton**

Bond, Brian (Ed.), *Victorian Military Campaigns* (1967)

Cook, H.C.B., *The Sikh Wars* (1975) – **Gough, Smith, Campbell, C. & R.Napier, Nicholson, McCabe**

Dictionary of National Biography

Farwell, Byron, *Eminent Victorian Soldiers* (1985)

Hannah, W.H., *Bobs; Kipling's General* (1972) – **Roberts**

Haythornthwaite, Philip, *Colonial Wars Source Book* (1995)

Hibbert, Christopher, *The Destruction of Lord Raglan* (1961)

Hibbert, Christopher, *The Great Mutiny: India, 1857* (1978)

Lehmann, John, *Remember You Are An Englishman: Biography of Sir Harry Smith* (1977)

Lehmann, John, *All Sir Garnet: Life of Lord Wolseley* (1964)

Magnus, Philip, *Kitchener* (1958)

Mercer, Patrick, *Give Them A Volley and Charge: Inkerman, 1854* (1998) – **Raglan, Cathcart, Pennefather, Haines**

Montgomery, John, *Toll for the Brave* (1963) – **MacDonald**

Myatt, Frederick, *The March to Magdala* (1970) – **R.Napier**

Napier, Priscilla, *Revolution and the Napier Brothers* (1973)

Napier, Priscilla, *I have Sind: Charles Napier, India, 1841-44* (1990)

Napier, Priscilla, *Raven Castle: Charles Napier, India, 1844-51* (1991)

Pakenham, Thomas, *The Boer War* (1979)

Pearson, Hesketh, *The Hero of Delhi: Life of John Nicholson* (1939)

Pollock, J.C., *Way to Glory: Life of Havelock of Lucknow* (1957)

Powell, G., *Buller, a Scapegoat?* (1994)

Preston, Adrian (ed.), *In Relief of Gordon: Wolseley's Campaign Journal, 1884-85* (1967)

Roberts, F-M Lord, VC, etc., *Forty-One Years in India* (1900)

Sweetman, John, *Raglan* (1993)

Wolseley, Viscount, *Story of a Soldier's Life* (1903)

Wood, F-M Sir Evelyn, VC, etc., *From Midshipman to Field-Marshal*, 2 Vols. (1906)

THE PLATES

Note that ranks and decorations given below are those held by the individuals concerned at the time they are depicted.

A: GENERAL OFFICERS' FULL DRESS
A1: Major-General, CB, c.1840
A2: General, GCB, c.1870
A3: Lieutenant-General, KCB, c.1900
This plate shows the full dress worn by general officers at different stages of the Victorian era, affording a contrast with the campaign dress adopted by those generals featured on the other plates. The feathered cocked hat remained the generals' headdress throughout the period, though with minor variations. It was replaced overseas by the foreign service helmet, with feathers, from c.1880, as in A3. A1's coatee, with buttons spaced according to rank, gave way from 1855 to the tunic of A2 and later of A3, with varying embellishments. The sash, in a wider, shoulder version from 1855, reverted to the waist from 1880. Knee boots, when mounted, were adopted from the mid-1870s.

Generals' swords had a mameluke hilt throughout the period.

B: INDIA, 1843
B1: Major-General Sir Charles Napier, KCB
B2: Officer, Honourable East India Company Bombay Horse Artillery
B3: Sowar, Honourable East India Company Sind Irregular Horse
Napier is depicted here during his conquest of Sind, based on contemporary portraits, an 1848 photograph, and two paintings of his Sind victories by George Jones. In the latter, of which Napier approved, he wears an oilskin-covered forage cap, though he sometimes wore a white headdress. Over his undress frock coat, with buttons in pairs for a major-general, and aiguillette arranged somewhat eccentrically as was his wont, he wears a *poshteen* - the goatskin coat of the Frontier, also worn by B3. His jack boots over loose white trousers are non-regulation. His native *tulwar* replaces a regulation general's sword.

Unlike his commander, B2 is dressed as per regulations which, apart from the helmet, resembled the Royal Horse Artillery's. The Sind Horse, B3, being irregular cavalry, had a more indigenous costume of turban, *alkalak*, *pyjama* trousers and jack boots.

C: INDIA, 1846
C1: General Sir Hugh Gough, GCB
C2: Major-General Sir Harry Smith, KCB
C3: Sergeant Bernard McCabe, HM 31st Regiment
Sergeant McCabe is here being presented by his divisional commander, Sir Harry Smith, to his C in C, Sir Hugh Gough, after his act of gallantry on the battlefield of Sobraon, 10 February 1846. Gough and Smith both wear general officers' undress frock coats, with rank distinguished by the button spacing. Over his frock Gough wears his famous 'white fighting coat' with his white hat, as shown in Sir Francis Grant's portrait. Smith wears his undress forage cap with white cover. McCabe has a similar headdress, worn with his regimental undress shell jacket, with Light Company

distinctions, and the accoutrements of the period, plus the waistbelt often worn in India.

All wear Oxford-mixture trousers.

D: THE CRIMEA, 1854
D1: Lieutenant-Colonel Lacy Yea, HM 7th Royal Fusiliers
D2: Brigadier-General Hon. James Scarlett
D3: Lieutenant-General Hon. Sir George Cathcart, KCB
Yea is in his regimental field officer's dress uniform as worn on landing in the Crimea, before a more relaxed dress became customary.

Scarlett's dress, from Sir Francis Grant's portrait, is that worn when commanding the Heavy Brigade at Balaclava, with non-regulation helmet of his own design and a frock coat over his old 5th Dragoon Guards stable jacket. He has retained his Heavy Cavalry sword, 1822 pattern. Cathcart's oilskin-covered forage cap, frock coat, cloak, and trousers are as per 1846 Dress Regulations for generals' undress uniform. His non-regulation long boots were a relic of his South African campaigning in 1852-53.

Statue of Sir Colin Campbell (Lord Clyde) in his Mutiny dress, erected in George Square, Glasgow; a similar statue stands in Waterloo Place, London. See Plate G1. (T. Moles)

greatcoats; hence Haines' outer garment, of officers' pattern, worn with his regimental forage cap. His sword is suspended from his undress waistbelt with frog; and he has a privately-purchased revolver - the 1851 single-action Adams in .50cal was a popular choice.

F: THE INDIAN MUTINY, 1857-58

F1: Brigadier-General John Nicholson
F2: Major-General Sir Henry Havelock, KCB
F3: Major-General Sir Hope Grant, KCB

All three figures, in the varied costumes adopted in the Mutiny, are based on photographs, contemporary pictures and - for F1 - two statues. Nicholson's covered forage cap with curtain was a common Mutiny headdress. His khaki jacket (double-breasted in some sources) is non-regulation and must have been tailored to his own design. Havelock's portraits show different frock coats, the example illustrated being of post-1855 style and taken from a print signed and presumably sanctioned by him as correct. He and Grant have similar cap covers, based on T.J.Barker's Lucknow painting. This also includes Grant's loose clothing, from a photograph which also reveals that he retained his 9th Lancers' sword and sling-belt.

G: THE INDIAN MUTINY, 1857-58

G1: Lieutenant-General Sir Colin Campbell, GCB
G2: Brevet Lieutenant-Colonel John Ewart,
HM 93rd Highlanders
G3: Sergeant Joe Lee, HM 53rd Regiment

This plate depicts the Secunderbagh incident at Lucknow on 16 November 1857, described in the text section on Colin Campbell. Contemporary Mutiny pictures show Campbell in varying undress clothing; this is from a photograph, two portraits and statues. He wears one of the earliest sun helmets, with airpipe; and carries his sword in a shoulder belt of his own design, worn variously over and under his coat. Ewart wears a 'boat coat', issued at home to the 93rd for a China expedition before the regiment was diverted to India en route. As a mounted field officer he wears trews rather than a kilt. His broadsword was suspended from slings attached to a waistbelt under the coat. The 53rd Regiment with which 'Dobbin' Lee served relieved Lucknow in their home service tunics, but with locally-made trousers, and covered forage caps.

E: THE CRIMEA, 1854

E1: Major-General John Pennefather, CB
E2: General Lord Raglan, GCB
E3: Captain (Brevet LtCol) Frederick Haines,
HM 21st Royal North British Fusiliers

An Inkerman scene, with the battlefield commander Pennefather briefing his C-in-C Raglan, while Haines reports from the Barrier.

Pennefather and Raglan, both from photographs, are in frock coats of a slightly less formal style than the 1846 regulation type and commonly worn by Crimean War generals and staff. Raglan wears his dress hat, in contrast to Pennefather's forage cap, and carries his specially-adapted telescope to compensate for his missing right arm.

Most regiments, including the 21st, fought Inkerman in

ABOVE RIGHT **MajGen Sir Herbert Kitchener, KCB, KCMG, as Sirdar (C-in-C) of the Egyptian Army, which he commanded from 1892 to 1899. See Plate L1. (P.J.Haythornthwaite)**

RIGHT **LtCol R.M.Rogers, VC (bearded, seated centre, facing front) and officers of HM 90th LI in the Zulu War, 1879. See Plate H1. (Africana Museum)**

OPPOSITE **Field-Marshal Lord Roberts of Kandahar, VC, KP, GCB etc., aged nearly 68 in June 1900 when his army in South Africa entered Pretoria. Cartoon by Spy - cf Plate I1.**

H: JUNIOR COMMANDERS, 1860-97

H1: Lieutenant Robert Rogers, HM 44th Regiment; China, 1860
H2: Lieutenant Walter Hamilton, Queen's Own Corps of Guides (PFF); Kabul, 1879
H3: Lieutenant Haldane Rattray, 45th (Rattray's Sikhs), Bengal Infantry; NW Frontier, 1897

According to its divisional orders and LtCol H.H.Crealock's eyewitness drawings, the 44th attacked the Taku Forts in airpipe helmets and India-pattern scarlet frocks, as illustrated. Rogers' 1822-pattern infantry sword is suspended from his waistbelt slings.

Hamilton, from a photograph, wears regulation undress of the Guides' British officers, with his sword and revolver attached to an early version of the Sam Browne belt, invented by the eponymous Indian Army general, but without cross-strap. Rattray, from a photograph, is in the universal khaki drill service dress introduced in India from 1885, with canvas gaiters instead of the usual puttees, and the field service cap sometimes substituted off-duty for the helmet.

I: SECOND AFGHAN WAR, 1878

I1: Major-General Frederick Roberts, VC, CB
I2: Lieutenant-Colonel Francis Brownlow, HM 72nd Highlanders
I3: Sepoy, 5th Gurkha Regiment (PFF)

As this Peiwar Kotal scene exemplifies, khaki clothing was widely but not universally worn during the Second Afghan War (see MAA 198, pp.37-39). Roberts, from photographs, wears a khaki frock and breeches with riding boots and a *poshteen*. All ranks of the 72nd wore trews of Prince Charles Edward Stuart tartan; Brownlow, being a mounted field officer, has riding boots, other officers having tartan puttees. Both he and Roberts have white, khaki-covered helmets of a later (c.1870) design than H1's. Later in this war the 5th Gurkhas adopted khaki clothing but at Peiwar Kotal it fought in rifle-green with khaki puttees. The sepoy is armed with Snider rifle, bayonet and kukri.

J: AFRICA, 1868-84

J1: Lieutenant-General Sir Robert Napier, KCB; Abyssinia, 1868
J2: Major-General Sir Garnet Wolseley, KCMG, CB; Ashanti expedition, 1873
J3: Brigadier-General Sir Herbert Stewart, KCB; Sudan, 1884

Napier's dress is from a photograph taken in Abyssinia, where a variety of service clothing was worn. His helmet is of a non-universal pattern, most having the airpipe type. Wolseley wears the special dress he devised for all his Ashanti force, of Elcho-grey tweed, officers having Norfolk jackets of that material. He is armed with a revolver and the Elcho sword bayonet which he recommended instead of a sword. (See MAA 198, pp.35-37, for this and Abyssinia).

Stewart and all his Camel Regiments had grey serge frocks, cord breeches, riding boots or puttees. He is armed with a revolver and his former regiment's Heavy Cavalry sword.

K: ZULULAND, 1879

K1: Colonel Evelyn Wood, VC
K2: Lieutenant-Colonel Redvers Buller
K3: Bugler Walkinshaw, 90th Light Infantry

Although promoted full colonel as a Zululand column commander, Wood retained his 90th LI undress frock, with khaki-dyed helmet, as shown in photographs and LtCol J.N.Crealock's watercolours. The latter and a W.Fairlie sketch are the sources for Buller's near-civilian outfit of 'wideawake' hat and Norfolk jacket, more appropriate for his Frontier Light Horse than his 60th Rifles' uniform. Walkinshaw's dress is from a photograph of Wood's bodyguard of 90th mounted infantrymen. He is armed with a Swinburne-Henry carbine.

L: SUDAN, 1898

L1: Major-General Sir Herbert Kitchener, KCB, KCMG
L2: Colonel Hector MacDonald, DSO
L3: Askari, Xth Sudanese Battalion, Egyptian Army

Both Kitchener and MacDonald wear khaki drill service dress introduced for overseas from 1896 in emulation of the Indian practice adopted from 1885. Both have the new 'Wolseley' helmet worn only by officers in the 1898 Sudan campaign. In contrast to Kitchener's riding boots, MacDonald wears 'Stohwasser' gaiters. In some Omdurman photographs Kitchener's khaki drill appears bleached to a very pale, near-white colour. The *askari's* khaki-covered red *tarbush*, jersey and other kit are based - as are all these figures - on photographs, and G.D.Giles' painting, of scenes after the Atbara victory. Egyptian Army infantry were armed with Martini-Henry rifles, not the British infantry's Lee-Metford.

INDEX

COMPANION SERIES FROM OSPREY

MEN-AT-ARMS
An unrivalled source of information on the organisation, uniforms and equipment of the world's fighting men, past and present. The series covers hundreds of subjects spanning 5,000 years of history. Each 48-page book includes concise texts packed with specific information, some 40 photos, maps and diagrams, and eight colour plates of uniformed figures.

WARRIOR
Definitive analysis of the appearance, weapons, equipment, tactics, character and conditions of service of the individual fighting man throughout history. Each 64-page book includes full-colour uniform studies in close detail, and sectional artwork of the soldier's equipment.

ORDER OF BATTLE
The most detailed information ever published on the units which fought history's great battles. Each 96-page book contains comprehensive organisation diagrams supported by ultra-detailed colour maps. Each title also includes a large fold-out base map.

CAMPAIGN
Concise, authoritative accounts of history's decisive military encounters. Each 96-page book contains over 90 illustrations including maps, orders of battle, colour plates, and three-dimensional battle maps.

NEW VANGUARD
Comprehensive histories of the design, development and operational use of the world's armoured vehicles and artillery. Each 48-page book contains eight pages of full-colour artwork including a detailed cutaway.

AIRCRAFT OF THE ACES
Focuses exclusively on the elite pilots of major air campaigns, and includes unique interviews with surviving aces sourced specifically for each volume. Each 96-page volume contains up to 40 specially commissioned artworks, unit listings, new scale plans and the best archival photography available.

COMBAT AIRCRAFT
Technical information from the world's leading aviation writers on the century's most significant military aircraft. Each 96-page volume contains up to 40 specially commissioned artworks, unit listings, new scale plans and the best archival photography available.